The Irresistible Introvert

The Irresistible Introvert

Harness the Power of Quiet Charisma in a Loud World

Michaela Chung

Skyhorse Publishing

Skyhorse Publishing books may be purchased in bulk at special discounts for sales promotion, corporate gifts, fund-raising, or educational purposes. Special editions can also be created to specifications. For details, contactthe Special Sales Department, Skyhorse Publishing, 307 West 36th Street, 11th Floor, New York, NY 10018 or info@skyhorsepublishing.com.

Skyhorse® and Skyhorse Publishing® are registered trademarks of Skyhorse Publishing, Inc.®, a Delaware corporation.

Visit our website at www.skyhorsepublishing.com.

10 9 8 7 6 5 4 3 2 1

Library of Congress Cataloging-in-Publication Data is available on file.

Cover design by Rain Saukas

Print ISBN: 978-1-5107-0478-7

Ebook ISBN: 978-1-5107-0479-4

Printed in the United States of America

Contents

Introduction

"Why do you always disappear like that?" my friend asked. "I had no idea where you were."

By fifteen, I had been wandering off for as long as I could remember. To me, it was as natural as daydreaming. Now my friend was telling me that she had noticed my disappearing acts, and it bothered her. My invisibility cloak wasn't working as well as I thought it was. What else had others noticed about me that wasn't to their liking?

I already sensed that I was different, but it wasn't until high school that people began to comment on it. "You're really quiet," they said. "What's wrong?" Usually nothing was wrong; I was happily fantasizing, or observing. After a while, though, I began to think that they were right. Maybe there was something inherently wrong with me. I would later learn that about one-third to one-half of the world's population feels just as flawed and misunderstood as I was. But we'll get to that later.

There was something else about my teenage years that I think I should mention. After the awkward puberty years passed, there was a certain comment I received even more often than "you're quiet." Once again, my invisibility cloak was failing and people were eager to tell me their observations about me. This time, what they had to say was more complimentary. People were telling me I was beautiful by the time I entered high school. I had a pretty face, good hair, nice eyes—great! According to the popular shows at the time (*Dawson's Creek*;

Party of Five; Beverly Hills, 90210), being beautiful was the ultimate VIP pass. It got you into the cool crowd and made boys like you. More importantly, it gave you something to work with. Beauty was a winning hand to play when love and acceptance were on the table. However, when I still felt like an outsider among my peers despite my outward beauty, I was left to wonder: *Do I have an ugly personality?*

Our culture is great at reinforcing the idea that an introverted personality is unattractive. Introversion has long been depicted as the ugly little sister of extroversion. To extroverts are attributed all the attractive qualities: charisma, friendliness, confidence. Meanwhile, introverts get the tattered hand-me-downs. We are labeled as withdrawn, antisocial, and depressed. A while ago I received an email from an introverted man from Switzerland named Claude. The story he shared sounded all too familiar:

> Yesterday, I started an English course. The first lesson was about "finding the real you." We had to match character adjectives with meanings 1-10. I had matched "introversion" with "self-reliant" and gave it a positive meaning. "No," said our teacher. "Introversion matches to withdrawn and is generally seen as negative. And extroversion is seen as positive." BAAH. It made me furious. Immediately felt that feeling of "something is wrong with me" again.

Stories like Claude's are quite common. With all the misconceptions about us, you would think that introverts are a small and freakish minority. As alluded to earlier, introverts make up roughly one-half to one-third of the world's population. Yet, the qualities that are as natural to us as breathing—the very same qualities that we share with millions of other introverts across the globe—make us feel defective. Just like me, many introverts come to believe that there is something wrong with them. I have received countless messages from introverts who say that they felt a sense of vindication after discovering their introversion. Somehow, learning that they are not the only ones who are quiet and inwardly inclined made them feel like it was finally okay to be who they were. They breathed a sigh of relief knowing that they were not strange or defective. They were simply introverts.

The most basic definition of an introvert is someone who gains energy by turning inward and loses energy in stimulating environments. Introverts are more easily overstimulated than extroverts. This is why we tend to enjoy contemplative, quiet activities. Meanwhile, extroverts prefer to direct their energies outward. They require more stimulation to feel good. This leads them to seek out busier environments that give them a buzz. Extroverts also tend to be risk-takers, while introverts are often risk-averse. In addition to our inward orientation, we introverts share several other qualities, preferences, and quirks.

Some introverted traits seem to be ingrained. Others are a result of the culture we live in. For example, many introverts have learned to cope with constant over stimulation by putting up a wall. This leads people to believe that introverts are cold or standoffish, but this is not our true nature.

The innate qualities that most introverts share are a love of introspection, a need for solitude, and a slower, more focused communication style.

Love of Introspection

Introspection is a favorite pastime for introverts. We love to explore the colorful landscapes of our imagination. Many of us have been criticized for our wandering minds. We've been told to get our head out of the clouds and stop daydreaming. What people don't understand is that there is a good reason for our inwardly focused ways. The outside world often feels like an assaulting force for introverts. At every turn there are energy vampires threatening to suck us dry. Turning inward is as much a means of survival as it is a source of comfort. Our love of introspection also brings meaning and direction to our life.

The Need for Solitude

An introvert's desire for solitude is more than just a preference. It is crucial to our health and happiness. We need time alone to restore ourselves. Introverts are pressured to push ourselves to the point of exhaustion in social situations—then we feel guilty for becoming irritable and grouchy. We blame ourselves for not being able to be "on" all the time. But when we give ourselves permission to seek the solitude we crave, life becomes lighter. Social situations are more bearable. Even annoying small talk is easier to endure when we've fortified ourselves with solitude.

A Different Approach to Communication

Introverts are known for being quiet. This can feel like a liability in the noisy world we live in. While extroverts are verbal processors, who speak as they think, introverts need to think before we speak. This leads to a slower, more thoughtful communication style that involves fewer words and longer pauses. We prefer to explore topics more in-depth, instead of flitting from subject to subject as many extroverts do. If the conversation doesn't interest us, we often go quiet and retreat into the wonderland that is our imagination. We find endless entertainment in our ideas and fantasies.

Other Introvert Idiosyncrasies

- Many introverts identify as highly sensitive
- Most introverts hate talking on the phone
- We are often spiritual
- We have a tendency to over think
- We prefer deep conversations over small talk
- We often write better than we speak

Of course, not every introvert will relate to all of the qualities I mention in this book. However, I have tried my best to share experiences and perspectives that most introverts can identify with. Likewise, my descriptions of extroverts are generalized and will not necessarily apply to every extrovert in every circumstance. We are all unique snowflakes with our own behaviors, habits, and traits. I highlight certain commonalities to help introverts see that we are not alone. Many others share the very qualities that made us think there is something wrong with us.

Introversion and extroversion occur on a spectrum. This means there are different degrees of introversion. No one person is completely an introvert or completely an extrovert. It is possible for us to have qualities that are associated with extroversion, such as a love of adrenaline-inducing adventures or a talkative, bubbly personality. Again, the main definition of introversion has to do with where we get our energy from. Introverts can be sociable and even outgoing, but we will need ample time to be alone and recharge our energy between social spurts.

Recently, my friend's colleague decided to take a vacation by herself. "Do you think you'll get lonely?" asked my friend.

"No. I'm taking my inner being with me," she replied, bending her arm as if carrying a parcel on her hip. The gesture made my friend giggle; however, being an introvert herself, she could relate to what her colleague was saying. People assume that introverts are lonely when we turn inward. In reality, we are lonelier when we spend too much time focusing outward. Turning in is both a joy and a necessity for introverts. We need to feel connected to our "inner being," which is comprised of our thoughts, feelings, unique perspectives, and intuition. Unfortunately, the world is eager to force us out—out of our head, out of our home, out of our shell—and onto Planet Extrovert.

There is a real bias toward extroversion in our culture. This leads introverts to give into the pressure to seek fulfillment on the outside. We think that doing as extroverts do will make us more attractive and likeable. Perhaps to some extent it will, but there are drawbacks. For one, we would attract the wrong people. These people only like us for our mask. What lies beneath our carefully constructed persona is the real treasure. The other problem with striving to keep up with extroverts is that it exhausts us. It makes us feel irritable, stressed out, and even depressed.

Introverts are happiest when we stay connected to our inner world. Doing so allows us to cultivate our own kind of charisma. This is not the kind of charisma that shouts for attention or tells the best jokes at a party. Nor is it a smooth-talking sort of charisma that always knows what to say. True charisma has to do with a person's ability to draw us in and hold our attention. Introverts can do this without saying a word. It all begins with reconnecting to our inner nature. That is why the first part of this book is focused on helping introverts come home to ourselves.

Once we have reconnected to our inner nature, developing charisma is more about revealing what is already there, rather than adding anything on. Part two of this book helps introverts peel back our extroverted persona to reveal the glowing, authentic self beneath. We actually let people catch a glimpse of the good stuff that we usually keep to ourselves. One of the first things you'll learn in any creative writing class is to "show, don't tell." The extrovert's way is to tell. When it comes to sharing our inner irresistible, introverts are better off to show.

It's time for introverts to take off our invisibility cloak and show the world the beauty of our true personality. The best part is that we can do so in our own quiet way. No extroversion required.

Part 1

Coming Home to Yourself

1

The Extrovert's Way—a Road Map to Nowhere

As far as I can remember, I've always felt different. I was not normal; I was "other." Even at four years old I knew I didn't fit in. No matter what section of the kindergarten circle I sat at, I always felt like an outsider. It was as if everyone else had received a secret memo that I had missed. Eventually, though, I got the message. It went something like this:

> Dear Michaela,
>
> If you would like to be accepted into our private Circle of Normal People, there are some rules you must follow.
>
> • You are required to spend plenty of time with others. It is not acceptable to sit together in silence. You must be having a conversation or doing some sort of activity—preferably both at the same time. Silence is permitted if you are playing sports, provided that you converse before and after the game. We also highly recommend that you join your teammates for a postgame chocolate sundae or Coca-Cola float.

- You must go out and socialize on weekends. Staying home on a weeknight is permissible, but socializing on Friday and Saturday is absolutely essential. Acceptance into the Circle hinges on how well you follow this rule. Acceptable excuses for failing to obey this rule include: contagious illness, injury, a family emergency or death, final exams, or your own death.

- You must accept that constant noise will be a part of your life from now on. Don't bother trying to tell others to speak more quietly or to turn down the volume on the stereo. This will make both you and the Circle seem very uncool and will lead to your immediate demotion in status. Repeated anti-noise infractions could result in your expulsion from the Circle.

- The Circle of Normal People prides itself on the popularity of its members. One, two, or even three friends is not sufficient. Ten is adequate. Over twenty is preferred. It is not necessary to spend one-on-one time with each person, so long as you can remember one another's names most of the time and make small talk as needed.

- Toughen up, dammit. You must never let people see your weaknesses, especially if said weaknesses could be labeled as timid, wimpy, or sissy-like. Crying in public is out of the question.

If you are able to abide by the above restrictions, we would be happy to have you as a member of the Circle of Normal People. The benefits of membership

include: exemption from ridicule from other Circle members, liberation from the burden of thinking for yourself, a free birthday meal at Denny's.
Sincerely,
Norm Al Pearson

In our culture, extroversion is considered the norm. It is the club that everyone wants to be part of. A lot of people think it's the superior personality type. Countless times, when I have told people that I am a writer and coach for introverts, they've asked, "So, you teach them how to be extroverted?" I fight back an eye roll and tell them that is most definitely *not* what I do.

Before we go any further, I want to get one thing straight. Extroverts are not superior to introverts, and vice versa. We are different personality types with different needs and motivations. In our culture, different is scary. Extroverts have laid claim on the definition of normal, leaving introverts to feel guilty for not fitting in.

While I was in college, I spent several months living with extended family members who were close in age to me. Every night, the four of us ate dinner together. Most of the time, the others carried on chatting after the meal. Meanwhile, I slipped away to my room to do homework or read. One day, one of the other women in the house pulled me aside to tell me that I had deeply offended her. She said that it was "very rude" that I didn't stay and chat with the others after dinner. I was shocked. I thought it was enough that we ate together every single night. Now she was telling me I had to linger and talk for a half hour? What next? Would we have to join hands and sing "Kumbaya" before brushing our teeth? *Come on.*

Even though I thought she was being ridiculous, I couldn't help but feel bad. My sensitive guilt reflex had been triggered, and I was queasy with shame. I felt like a little kid being scolded for something as natural as falling asleep at naptime. I didn't know whether to argue, laugh, or cry. Like most introverts, I hate conflict. So, I slithered away to my room like the green scaly creature I imagined I was. And I cried.

Experiences like the one I just shared send a very strong message to introverts. Our way is right. Your way is wrong. The right way, of course, is the extrovert's way.

The Extrovert's Way

If happiness is a destination, extroverts are in the fast lane. They need more stimulation to feel good compared to introverts, so they tend to talk and move at a faster pace. They want to do it all, see it all, and say it all with as few rest stops as possible. The extrovert's way wouldn't be so bad if introverts felt like it was optional. Extroverts could carry on doing what extroverts do best. Meanwhile, we introverts could make our own path.

Sometimes, we do want to take a little road trip into extrovert territory. But we would like to be able to pick and choose our extroverted endeavors. Ideally, we would approach life like a buffet, helping ourselves to a small side of meet and greet, a healthy dollop of deep thought, and a sprinkling of social fluff. No one would judge or criticize what we put on our plate. They would let us have our slice of solitude, and eat it too. This is not how it goes for most introverts. Instead, we are deemed inferior the moment we navigate away from the extrovert's definition of normal.

There are plenty of people out there who are as knowledgeable about introversion as mosquitos are about long division.

Such people tell us that introversion is a deficiency that needs to be fixed. Extroversion is the standard to shoot for. From an early age, introverts receive the message that to be popular, successful, and attractive, you must be extroverted. In childhood we notice that smiley, talkative children are favored. As teens, our hormones beg us to try on a more attention-grabbing personality. If we don't succumb to the pressure to change in our youth, we are certain to do so in adulthood. Many of us have done everything society has told us to do; yet we feel more lost than ever. This is because the extrovert's way has led us astray.

You've likely experienced the impact of the extrovert's way in your own life. Here are a few scenarios that might sound familiar.

Scenario #1: You want to spend Saturday night at home alone with a good book, but your friends—and society as a whole—tell you this is not normal. To them, the path to a happy and fulfilling life is paved with barbecues, parties, and lots of nights out on the town.

Scenario #2: You are at a barbecue and you are starting to fade. You want to leave early, or at least go for a walk so you can recharge; however, others say it's weird to go off on your own when there is laughter and fun times to be had. They tell you the only way to enjoy life is to join the party.

Scenario #3: You have two best friends with whom you spend most of your time, and you have no desire to make more. But your friends, family, and all those happy people in Bud Light commercials tell you that more friends equals more happiness. Surrounding yourself with lots of people is the only way to feel fulfilled.

There is a common theme among these scenarios: the key to happiness is to surround ourselves with people all the time. The thing about the extrovert's way of socializing is that simply being around people is not enough. If it were, introverts might have an easier time. Instead, socializing is treated like a sport. We have to show up in our extrovert's uniform prepared to be jostled and judged by the other team. From the moment we step on the field, the other guys are sizing us up. They wonder if we can hold our own in a conversation match. We wonder if we'll still be standing after a full hour of banter back and forth. By halftime our extrovert's uniform is unraveling. We feel embarrassed when our introverted underpants begin to show through. Socializing in this way makes us feel like losers. No matter how much we try, we can't win. And believe me, we've tried.

That's what a lot of extroverts don't understand when they nonchalantly say things like, "C'mon, try to live a little." Or when they roll their eyes when we express our desire to stay home, as if we are just being lazy and not trying. We have tried. Oh, yes, we have tried, and tried, and tried to turn ourselves into extroverts, to no avail. No matter how much we would like to enjoy being around other humans 24/7, we just don't. This doesn't mean we hate people, nor does it mean we're lazy. What it means is that we need alone time as much as we need human contact—sometimes more so.

Forcing ourselves to be around people all the time can have severe consequences for introverts. It often leads to feelings of depletion, sadness, and even depression. In a *Mamamia* article, "This Is Who I Am, Deal with It," Wendy Squires talks about how her forced extroversion triggered her depression.

> What I see now . . . was that I was not allowing myself time to recharge, to be alone, to say nothing

and just be after socially active periods. Instead, I would believe such plateaus were a depression descending which, dammit, I refused to accept or needed to block, forcing me out the door and back to people and alcohol and the pressure to be up— the very triggers that shot me down in the first place.

Squires thought her need for alone time was a sign of depression. In the end, it was a lack of solitude that triggered her descent into depression. Like Squires, many introverts receive the wrong message about solitude.

Our extroverted culture makes introverts feel despicable for wanting to be alone. Like thieves snatching something that doesn't belong to them, we have to "steal" a moment of solitude. If only introverts could see that we have a right to our alone time. We have a right to enjoy it too.

Think vs. Do

The trouble is that the extroverts in our lives don't understand our need for alone time. "But what are you going *do* at home by yourself?" they ask. "Won't you be bored?" If I had to summarize an extrovert's approach to life in one word, I would choose "do." For introverts, it would be "think." Of course, extroverts can think and introverts can do. But for introverts, thinking is a form of doing. Extroverts don't usually get this; their doing is more literal. They go out, meet friends, run errands, and get big and important things done. They don't see much value in all our reflecting and introspecting. To them, it just looks like we are sitting around doing nothing. In our productivity-obsessed culture, taking time to sit alone and reflect is like riding the bench while your team is playing the World Series. The extroverts are the ones running around on the field, swinging hard, and stealing bases. They get all the high fives, all the glory. Few people understand that a lot can be accomplished while sitting on the sidelines. As we observe, we notice patterns and learn from the mistakes of other players. Sitting out for a while also allows us to store up energy, so we can play our best when we do make it onto the field.

Sensitivity Is Synonymous with Weakness

In the extrovert's World Series, introverts are seen as the weakest link. This is not just because of our need to be alone. Our sensitivity is also seen as a weakness. According to Dr. Elaine Aron, author of *The Highly Sensitive Person: How to Thrive when the World Overwhelms You,* a highly sensitive person (HSP) has a sensitive nervous system. Highly stimulating environments easily overwhelm them. Although not all introverts are highly sensitive, most HSPs (about 70 percent) are introverted.

Sensitivity comes with many gifts, such as strong intuition, empathy, and an appreciation for subtlety. Despite our strengths, sensitive introverts struggle with the extrovert's way. Since extroverts actively seek out more stimulation, they are perplexed by our desire to avoid it. They don't understand why their constant need to turn up the volume on life would upset us. I once had a roommate—we'll call him Joe—who loved to blast electronic music first thing in the morning. His personality was just as loud and up-tempo as the stuff blaring from his stereo. He could talk for hours, often clapping his hands or pounding his fists for emphasis. Even though I liked Joe, I found living with him exhausting. His noisy way of life was too much for my sensitive nervous system. I spent much of my time hiding in my room.

The More-Is-More Mentality

It's not just noise that makes introverts want to dim the lights and hide for days. Our culture's obsession with always accumulating more is just as overwhelming. Bigger is better! Go big or go home! Supersize me, baby! These are household phrases that appeal to extroverted households. The quest for more—more things, more entertainment, more stimulation—is very much an extrovert's pursuit. Even though we don't fully understand it, introverts can easily get sucked in by the extrovert's more-is-more mentality. If there weren't so much pressure to acquire and consume, most introverts would be happy to live with less. Often, as long as we have our books, our imagination, and a wide slice of solitude, we're content.

My theory is that introverts give energy to everything we own. With this in mind, we had better be sure our possessions offer us something valuable in return. Inanimate objects aren't as generous as society would have us believe. They can't love us or make us feel less lonely at night. Some stuff has a real practical purpose in our daily life, while other objects are just there to amuse or impress. Since introverts find plenty of amusement in our own mind, we're better off foregoing possessions that don't serve us in some immediate way. Some people would find this view too extreme to take seriously. For such people, acquisition is the purpose of life. More stuff equals more success.

Another way success is measured in our culture is by the number of friends we have. Never mind if these friends have no idea where we went to middle school or how we like our tea in the morning. As long as there is a decent sized crowd at our funeral, we'd have lived a good life. (Funny how even death doesn't put an end to the popularity contest.) Introverts prefer to take a quality-over-quantity approach to relationships. This means that we tend to have fewer friends and fewer lovers over a lifetime. Besides those nerve-racking adolescent years when being popular is the only thing that matters, we aren't too concerned with having a ton of friends. Managing too many friendships is stressful for introverts. Meanwhile, extroverts love having lots of friends. Friends offer an endless supply of fun, and, as the old saying (coined by the English writer John Heywood, who was probably an extrovert) goes, "The more, the merrier!"

I've hardly ever heard an introvert say "the more, the merrier" and actually mean it. If we do utter these evil four words, it is through clenched teeth. Instead of feeling merry in large groups, we often feel more alone. This quote by Henry Rollins says it best: "Yes, I guess you could say I'm a loner, but I feel more lonely in a crowded room with boring people than I feel on my own."

The Open-Door Policy

One of the things that irked me about living with my extroverted roommate, Joe, was that he had an open-door policy with all of his friends. They could show up at nearly any hour of the day, and he would greet them with sickening enthusiasm.

I'm not so into the open-door policy, especially during work hours. I can understand keeping the door open sometimes, but all the time? I'd rather not spend my days knowing that, at any moment, someone could barrel into my office like a bulldozer and demolish my train of thought. Since I work for myself, I can enforce a closed-door policy without reprimand. Many introverts don't have this luxury. They work in offices that force employees to keep the door open at all times—that is, if they have a door at all. Nowadays, a lot of companies embrace open office plans. I have worked for such a company and found it hard to concentrate. People were constantly stopping by my desk to ask questions or make small talk.

Multitasking extroverts seem unfazed by the constant distractions of an open plan office. Like many introverts, I have never been good at multitasking. Introverts accomplish more when we can give our complete focus to a task without interruption. After years of exalting multitasking as the ultimate form of productivity, researchers are now finding that single-tasking introverts had it right all along. A group of Stanford researchers found that people who are media multitaskers do not pay attention, control their memory, or switch from one job to another as well as those who complete one task at a time. The researchers split one hundred students into two groups, those who regularly do a lot of media multitasking and those who don't. The researchers expected the multitaskers to have an edge, but their findings showed otherwise. "We kept looking for what they're better at, and we didn't find it," said Eyal Ophir, the study's lead author. It turns out that an introvert's focused approach is better for both the brain. The bottom line—yet another reason to keep the door closed.

Saying "No" to Normal

Now that I've spent some time in the Circle of Normal People, I can see that membership is not what I thought it would be. The price is too high for the supposed benefits. We are expected to give up our precious solitude, our love of being alone, our long walks through deep forests of thought. In return, we get to be part of something bigger than ourselves. That's the dream, right? The problem is that this "something bigger" is too big.

It crashes down on us like an anvil, crushing our soul in the process. With all this in mind, I've decided not to renew my membership in the Circle. But, I didn't want to leave without sending a message to our old friend Norm Al Pearson:

> Dear Norm,
>
> While I appreciate your offer to include me in your Circle, I am unable to accept your terms. I like thinking for myself. The moment I truly started doing so, I realized that your club is overrated. Its benefits are nothing but a myth bolstered by the bragging of its members.
>
> I'll take my Saturday nights in solitude over being a so-called "Normal Person" any day.
> Sincerely,
> Michaela

Just like the Circle of Normal People, the extrovert's way does not have nearly as many benefits as we are led to believe. We think we will find fulfillment and acceptance. That somehow our hair will be shinier and our eyes will have that special sparkle. What we will get instead is a cookie-cutter life and a vague sense longing. Now that we know the extrovert's way is not all it's cracked up to be for the many of us with more introverted personalities, we are free to choose a new direction. The best place to start is by turning inward.

2

The Way Out Is In: Finding Your Inner Compass

We shall not cease from exploration
And the end of all our exploring
Will be to arrive where we started
And know the place for the first time.

—*T. S. Eliot*

When I think about an introvert's true nature—their personality, natural preferences, gifts, and worldview—I imagine a treasure chest surrounded by fog. Some of us find our way through the fog faster than others. It took me about twenty-eight years to come home to myself. I took the first step by doing what we introverts do best: I turned in toward myself. Before I turned inward, however, I did what most "well-behaved" North American introverts do: I directed all my energy outward.

Like fish out of water, introverts are quiet people in a noisy world. We're told that growing sturdier limbs and a thicker skin is the only way to "make it," so we toughen up and force ourselves out of our comfort zone in the hopes that we will find happiness on the outside. If you had a pet goldfish as a child, you've probably seen what happens to fish out of water. They flounder and flail, convulsing on the floor as if suffering from a heart attack. The strange thing is that many goldfish voluntarily launch themselves out of their bowls. Goldfish suicide is a real phenomenon nowadays. Introverts are often just as eager to escape from our true nature.

I spent most of my twenties searching for meaning in external hobbies and achievements. I was a bank teller by day and a competitive salsa dancer by night. I planned dance events, hosted parties, and spent most weekends running errands or visiting friends. I did everything I could to "put myself out there" as I knew this was the best way to be a happy and well-adjusted citizen on Planet Extrovert. The trouble is that introverts are naturally oriented to our inner world of thoughts and feelings. We are internal processors, which means that our point of reference for relating to the world comes from within. In contrast, extroverts rely more heavily on external stimuli to inform their views and decisions. My outward focus went against my true nature. In my relentless search for fulfillment, I had forgotten a crucial navigation tool: my inner compass. Luckily, I didn't get so far off course that I completely lost touch with my intuition. I was connected to my inner voice just enough to hear it whisper that something was missing.

Since I had already searched outside myself for fulfillment in nearly every possible way, I thought, why not up the ante? I decided to quit my job and sell everything that wouldn't fit in a suitcase. Then I set out on a journey across three continents in search of my life's purpose. I wanted to locate the elusive intersection where my unique gifts and experiences collided with something the world needed. I hated it when people asked if I was trying to "find myself" because this made me sound like a cliché, but really, that was exactly what I was doing. I was like a little kid on a scavenger hunt, scuttling over rocks and lifting logs, hoping to find something that had been in my pocket all along. Eventually, I did find what I was looking for. I found shreds of it in every country I visited (there were seven in total: Australia, New Zealand, the United States, Mexico, Costa Rica, Panama, and Colombia) during my yearlong odyssey.

The place where I truly came home to myself was much less exotic than expected—my inner, authentic self. She had been waiting patiently for me to put down my suitcase, quit distracting myself with outward pursuits, and return to join her in her natural habitat.

The Introvert's Homeland

"Your solitude will be a support and a home for you, even
in the midst of very unfamiliar circumstances, and from
it you will find all your paths."

—Rainer Maria Rilke

Coming home to ourselves starts with turning down the volume around us. For quiet, sensitive souls, solitude is the golden thread that unites us with our inner world. Empty spaces and closed doors should be nonnegotiable for introverts. We need quiet to connect the dots in our constellations of thought. Sadly, introverts have been told to run from quiet comforts, rather than take pleasure in them. Our culture does not encourage or support the pursuit of solitude.

You may have a childhood memory of seeking solitude in nature, as you made tree forts or played imaginary games in the forest. Perhaps you searched for solitude within the pages of your favorite book. If you were fortunate enough to have a room of your own growing up, you spent countless hours there, quietly absorbed in solitary play. Your version of play might have looked different than that of your peers and siblings. I was raised with two older brothers, who played together like puppies. Meanwhile, I spent much of my time by myself, writing stories or dressing up dolls.

If you were like me, you were lucky enough to have a family who, for the most part, let you have your quiet comforts. If you were not so lucky, your love of being alone was a source of worry for your parents. To them, a happy childhood meant lots of activities, laughter, and horsing around. Your parents probably did not understand that you were perfectly happy in your quiet state. They could not believe what they did not see. Since your contentment was more of an inner glow than an outward display, they assumed you must be unhappy. Perhaps this led them to force you out the door and into places where you could make friends and have their version of fun. If you were really, really unlucky, your parents might even have feared your love of solitude was a sign that you had some kind of disorder. So, between playdates and soccer matches, they ushered you off to the psychiatrist's office to get a diagnosis for your quietness. Their worried actions gave you your first glimpse into the anti-quiet, anti-solitude, anti-anything-that-is-not-productive mind-set that dominates Western society.

As adults, we are fully steeped in the hot mess of an anti-solitude culture. We live in noisy environments with even noisier people. We lead lifestyles that are more conducive to chaos than quiet. Before we even leave our house, we can see the demands of the day stretched out in front of us like a freeway at 5:00 p.m. I frequently felt this way when I worked at one of the offices of a major mining company in Australia. Every day, I would get on a crowded bus to go to my big, shiny office building in the heart of Brisbane's central business district (CBD). By the time I reached the CBD, the streets were already bustling with people. The chaos was audible. It sounded like moaning metal and empty chatter. All the racket around me threw my inner world into turmoil. On the outside, I appeared calm and put-together, but internally I felt fragmented. That's the thing about introverts; we wear our chaos on the inside where no one can see it.

In the end, I decided to leave my contract early. The pay was not worth the stress of having scrambled insides. Other introverts might find themselves in a similar situation, but decide to stay put. Realistically, we can't all spend our days sitting in lotus position in a soundproof bubble. Thankfully, it is possible to withstand the demands of a loud world if we create pockets of quiet within the chaos. We can learn to hopscotch through the madness and find our footing in solitude. The first step is to change our relationship with silence.

The Right to Remain Silent

In a world of nonstop noise, silence is a real treat, especially when shared. In her book *The Art of Asking: Or How I Learned to Stop Worrying and Let People Help*, Amanda Palmer tells a story about a silent dinner she shared with her husband, author Neil Gaiman. While at a candlelit restaurant, the couple decided to forego talking and, instead, wrote notes to one another throughout the meal. "[B]y the end of the meal we'd shared a degree of intimate information that we probably wouldn't have if we'd just been sitting and chatting," says Palmer.

So, a married couple shared a meal in silence, passed a few notes—what's the big deal? There are plenty of other couples that share meals in silence. I see them all the time. The husband leafs through his newspaper while the wife stares into her phone. Neither says a single word. Here is another familiar scenario: the wife or girlfriend is mad, so she sits in a kind of silent protest, while the man keeps his head down and his mouth shut. The underlying message in these scenarios is that silence equals disinterest, anger, or apathy. However, silence can mean something very different for introverts.

Far from being bored in silence, introverts are often absorbed in a world of colorful thoughts. We are eager for the pause because it gives us the chance to mentally digest what we have seen and heard. If others didn't find silence so awkward, we could actually enjoy these moments of quiet. But, alas, this is not the case.

Our culture fears silence. Gaps in conversation are quickly filled with fluffy banter. The silent spaces in the day are crowded out by constant noise pollution. This aversion to quiet is a worldwide epidemic. During my travels I discovered it is especially obvious in highly extroverted cultures, such as those in Latin American countries. During my yearlong journey, I spent two months in Colombia, a country known for its vibrant people and landscapes. The entire nation seemed to be in a constant state of celebration and gyration. Even in the wee hours of the morning, the residue of laughter and music lingered in the hot air. At times, it felt like every inch of space was saturated with noise.

During my first week in Colombia, I took a bus from Turbo to Medellin. It was an eight-hour ride with a late-night arrival time, so I planned on sleeping during the last half of the journey. I experienced a rude awakening (literally) around 11:00 p.m. All the lights and televisions came on and salsa music blasted from every speaker. I looked around, irritated, expecting others to see the outrage of this late-night noise assault. But no one else seemed to mind. For them, blaring music was a welcome part of the ride. Like laughter and colorful conversation, music was meant to be shared. Silence was something to be avoided.

Sound dependency is rampant in North American culture too. We might be subtler about it, but we are just as eager to slaughter silence. Talking someone's ear off is normal; sitting in silence is awkward. We would rather have background noise follow us everywhere we go, rather than allow silence to take center stage.

I can understand the reasoning behind our culture's campaign against quiet. Silence feels uncomfortable if you're not used to it. In an impatient world of instant gratification, noise allows us to stay focused on the outside. Silence urges us to turn in. Even for introverts, the idea of turning inward can be frightening. It's as if we are lifting a giant rock that has never been moved—anything could be under there. We imagine a colony of dark critters leaping out at us or, even worse, a poisonous snake. Silence creates space for worry, self-criticism, and obsession to seep in. Snakes rarely strike above the ankle, but our thoughts go straight for the jugular.

It's not just our own critical thoughts that taunt us in the shadows of silence. The judgments and opinions of others reverberate through our memory, producing a flurry of guilt in their wake. Combined, these menacing thoughts create what I like to call the "Should Voice."

Turning Down the Should Voice

The Should Voice is comprised of all the things people tell us we *should* do to fit in. Introverts are overwhelmed by the never-ending list of "shoulds" that are doled out to us like candy from a young age:

"You should always say yes to an invitation."

"You should be open and friendly with acquaintances."

"You should play with the other children instead of playing alone."

"You should smile and be enthusiastic, even if you feel otherwise."

"You should engage in small talk and like it."

"You should be flirty and giggly like the other girls."

"You should be bold and gregarious like the other men."

"You should stay until the end of the party."

"You should come out of your shell."

"You should adopt a new personality because yours doesn't meet the status quo."

"You should not spend too much time alone or others will think you are boring or depressed."

Introverts hear these shoulds so often; they burrow their way into our psyche and overpower our inner voice. When we listen to the Should Voice we act out of obligation instead of conviction. We say "yes" to activities we would rather run from because disagreeing might be considered rude. Being agreeable is a form of self-preservation for introverts. Nodding our head takes less of our precious energy than voicing our true beliefs and opinions.

During my travels, I learned to live with less. My entire life fit into a small suitcase. My mental landscapes became more spare as well. The further I got away from the voices of my family, friends, and culture, the clearer my inner voice came through. If you could climb inside my head and do a comparison of what it looked like before and after my epic journey, you would find two very different spaces.

Pre-journey, my mind was cluttered with other people's expectations. Every time my own thoughts and beliefs looked for a place to sit and rest, they would find that the best seats were already taken by my father, mother, siblings, friends, acquaintances, and several other people whose names I've long since forgotten. My own thoughts had to hover in the back of the room like second-class citizens. Post-journey, far fewer people inhabited my headspace. My own thoughts got the best seats.

In the past, I had made decisions to please or impress others. With more freedom and time to myself, I started examining everything I believed. I also questioned my desires and feelings, listening carefully to find out if they belonged to me or somebody else who had been taking up precious real estate in my head. As more and more voices were evicted from my brain, making decisions became easier. The Should Voice no longer dictated my choices.

I've written about the Should Voice on my personal blog, Introvert Spring. On one blog post, a reader commented, "Currently working very, very hard to eliminate the word 'should' from my vocabulary (both internal and external), by replacing 'should' with 'could.' This is helping me to deal with my guilt and shame by being kinder to me." I love this. Acknowledging our power to choose is one of the kindest things we can do for ourselves. There is a big difference between saying "I should go out tonight" versus "I could go out tonight."

The first statement seems heavy, weighed down by guilt. The second statement is lighter and less daunting because the element of choice is present.

Once the Should Voice is silenced, introverts are faced with an important question: Who are you *really*? This is a tough one to answer. We know who people have told us we are ("you're quiet," "you're shy," "you're different"). We also know who people have told us we should be: someone who is outgoing, who likes to be around others a lot, and who enjoys going out and having fun. But who are you *really*?

The other night, I asked myself this question while lying awake in bed. I know who I am *not*. I am not nearly as complicated and serious as a lot of people think I am. Then again, I am not as superficial and shallow as many acquaintances assumed I was during my competitive salsa dancing days. It's a hard question to answer in the here and now after so many years of striving, comparing, and judging. So, I reached back into my memory and plucked a photograph that was taken when I was nine years old. I was wearing a floral dress (oh, how I loved dresses!) and my hair was tied back with a ribbon I had carefully chosen to match the violet flowers on my dress. The photo was taken in the backyard, a place where I had spent countless hours playing imaginary games, picking rhubarb, and taking my pet rat Mickey for "walks" (I hooked him up to a ferret leash and let him zigzag on the grass). Looking at this photograph made it easy to answer the question—I am a simple girl, who appreciates beauty.

What about you? Who are you *really*? You might have to reach into a far corner of your memory to find the answer. A little bit of time away from the crowd will help you to do this.

Retreat

Ironically, one of the best ways to move forward on our journey toward our true nature is to retreat. Although people usually think of a retreat as a getaway lasting at least two days, the key aspect of a retreat is simply to withdraw. For introverts, this could mean withdrawing into nature or into our room. We might also step back from our usual social circles so we can reconnect with our inner voice.

We don't need to find a cabin in the woods to go on a retreat. There are plenty of places to withdraw in our everyday environments. What matters most is that our mind has space to wander without too much interruption. A park bench, a quiet café, a public garden, a room with four walls—all these are wonderful spaces for a mini retreat. One of my favorite places to retreat to is a Thai restaurant near where I live. The room is spacious, and the atmosphere is simple and calm. One of the things I like most about this restaurant is how the employees treat me. They acknowledge and serve me with a polite warmth that is never imposing. Even though I'm a regular, they never ask me for my name or what I do. Some might view this as cold or sterile. Such people would prefer to go to the place "where everybody knows your name." However, for introverts seeking a sliver of solitude, a sense of anonymity is bliss.

Whether our retreat is mental or physical, it does not have to be a solitary act. With the right person, withdrawing in tandem is even more rejuvenating than it would be by ourselves. At the moment, I live in a quiet, little suite overlooking the ocean. Every morning I see an elderly man rowing past while his wife sits serenely across from him. I used to wonder where they were going, but then I realized that wasn't the point. Being on the water quenches their need for solitude. They are already exactly where they want to be—alone, together, on their daily retreat.

Self-care practices, such as retreats, are not just for special occasions. We need to incorporate weekly and daily restorative practices into our lives. Having a morning ritual of drinking tea in quiet is a great way for introverts to add a mini retreat to the day. Other ideas include:

- Going for a walk in nature
- Watching and/or playing with animals
- Bringing your full attention to eating a good meal
- Journaling
- Reading for pure pleasure
- Any kind of creative expression, such as photography, writing, drawing, or dancing
- Meditating

While retreats are wonderful, they are often too short-lived. Eventually, we must return to the real world. Whether returning from a thirty-minute lunch hour retreat or a week-long vacation, it's hard to come back. It is jarring to dive back into fast-paced environments after having some time to ourselves. It's best to slowly ease our way in.

Taking the Scenic Route

One of the by-products of an extrovert-dominated society is that everyone is always in a hurry. We feverishly race from one life milestone to the next, not even realizing that we are leaving ourselves behind in the process. I've noticed that my natural pace is much slower than the status quo. I walk, talk, and read slowly. Since slowness has many negative connotations in our culture (for example, stupidity, laziness, and lack of ambition), I used to feel self-conscious about my tortoise-like ways. For the sake of fitting in, I forced myself to speed up by rushing to meet my goals in a short time frame. In my early twenties, I was so determined to find my place in the world that I ran around in circles, like a dog chasing its tail. I changed school programs more often than most people change shoes. Later, I went through jobs and hobbies just as quickly. All my racing around only made me more confused about who I was, and where I was going in life.

For introverts, rushing through life feels a lot like running through thick mud. The faster we try to go, the more stuck we get. The sludge sucks at our feet, weighing down each step. If we pull away too forcefully, we launch ourselves right out of our boots. The only way to emerge from the muck is by taking slower, smaller steps.

Slowing down will feel like a relief for most introverts. Moving at a slower pace gives us time to process information more deeply. Sure, moving quickly allows us to do more, but without the opportunity to reflect on our activities, life loses its meaning. Another problem with trying to move too fast is that it exhausts us. We think we will accomplish more, but, in the end, we burn out, get sick, or become depressed—all of which are detrimental to our productivity. Slowing down is the scenic train ride through life. J. K. Rowling came up with the idea for the Harry Potter series while on a four-hour delayed train ride between Manchester and London. And it just so happens that the billionaire author's parents met on a train. They welcomed Rowling into the world a little over a year later. So, it seems that for J. K Rowling, and most other introverts, the scenic route is where the best ideas are conceived. This has certainly been the case for me.

Taking the First Step

Like Rowling, trains play a big role in my journey toward a more purposeful life. The idea to take the first step in my year-long odyssey came to me while sitting in the food court of one of Brisbane's busy train stations. I was in the thick of the fog at that point. I knew I didn't want to continue on the path I was on, but the alternative was still hazy. There were too many options to choose from. The uncertainty threatened to swallow me whole. *Where do I even begin?* I wondered, as I shoveled mouthfuls of takeaway butter chicken into my mouth. While I sat there stewing in my existential crisis, the answer appeared in an unlikely form.

A black-clad homeless man with body piercings seemed to come out of nowhere and pulled up the chair right next to mine. *God, why did he have to sit beside me?* I thought. There were plenty of other empty seats. Then he began drumming his fingers on the table. Now, I was really annoyed. I thought of getting up to leave, but before I could, he blurted out, "A journey of a thousand miles begins with one single step." I turned to him, confused. He pointed to one of the screens above the train schedule, and repeated, "Quote of the day: a journey of a thousand miles begins with one single step." Then he got up and walked away.

When I think of my yearlong odyssey of self-discovery, I always remember this experience as the invitation to take the first step. Beginning any new journey is scary. We are often more apt to stay stuck in the mud rather than brave the foggy realm of uncertainty. As we set out on the path toward our true nature, it helps to remember that we don't need to have all the answers right now. We just need to take the first step. Perhaps, this moment is your invitation to begin.

3

Navigating Energy Roadblocks

I once had a dream that a woman was stealing food right off my dinner plate. True to my introverted nature, I stayed calm on the outside, but on the inside, I was horrified. I felt the same sense of protectiveness over my meal as a prisoner must feel over his daily rations. People who grew up with several siblings will be familiar with the sense that there is never enough. At any moment you could run out of food and be left with a growling stomach. After waking from the dream, I realized this was how I felt as an introvert with limited energy supplies. I am acutely aware of the finite nature of my energy. I feel the need to guard it and ration it out carefully on an as-needed basis.

Inconsistent energy levels are one of the most frustrating obstacles we introverts face. If not for our sloth-like stamina, surely we would be as generous as Mother Teresa with our time and energy. We would feed the needy with our limitless enthusiasm. We would spend our days bouncing around from activity to activity as extroverts do. Surely, we would. Unfortunately, on most days we are barely able to sustain a hamster on our limited energy stores, let alone ourselves.

I might have been exaggerating with the Mother Teresa reference, but it's not entirely untrue. Introverts often have lofty goals. Our high expectations reach well beyond our average energy levels. It's frustrating to want to give, do, be, and achieve more than our energies permit. I am chronically delusional about how much I can accomplish in a short period of time. In high school, I was on students' council and the honor role. I played rugby, volunteered, and was heavily involved at my church. My can-do, go-getter attitude led to monthly meltdowns that my mother had come to expect. Nowadays, I pace myself. I've learned that I can actually accomplish more when I work with, rather than against, my energy cycles.

Honoring the Ebb and Flow of Energy

There is a natural ebb and flow to an introvert's energy. We are at our best when we work within these energy cycles. This is not always easy because we live in a culture of constant high tides. We're expected to always be up and about, bursting with endless energy for pointless busyness. The belief that our energy can and should always manifest in a Richard Simmons–like way is what causes drastic ups and downs. Our inevitable dips in energy are especially frustrating because we know what vitality feels like. When we're riding the high tides of our energy cycles, life is so much easier. We are sharper and more on top of things. Work goes more smoothly, and socializing is far less abrasive. If we could honor the fact that our relationships, work, and lives are cyclical in nature, our energy levels would become far more consistent.

The idea that we should always be "seizing the day" and "pushing through" is ridiculous. We have seasons for a reason. I realized this during my nomadic years of hopping from one warm country to the next. I traded Canadian white winters and burnt-orange autumns for an endless summer. Though this sounds amazing (and it was, much of the time), I missed the collective shift in mentality and energy that occurs at every change of season. I longed for that boost of motivation and productivity I felt each fall. I even began to recognize the value of winter. I hate the cold, but I love the creativity and intense focus I can cultivate during the colder months. A little hibernation is good for the mind.

Our energy cycles are especially obvious in our social lives. In this extrovert's world we live in, it is implied that busy is better, and the more activities we can cram into our week, the happier we'll be. This leads introverts to go out when every molecule in our being is crying for a night in. It also makes us feel bad for running out of social steam midway through the weekend, just as extroverts are hitting their stride. Unfortunately, most of the time our society's social speedometer only registers extrovert speed. Sometimes, we can keep up with the extroverts. But it is only so long before our energy levels drop and we need to turn inward again.

There are usually plenty of signs that we are entering into dangerously low energy levels. We become irritable and self-critical, overthinking our supposed shortcomings, and underestimating our value. Meanwhile, making conversation feels more and more laborious. Small talk is intolerable. After a while, people start to tell us we look zoned out. Despite all the obvious signs that it is time to take a break, some of us might push ourselves to continue at extrovert speed. Pushing too hard for too long inevitably leads to some kind of crash. We get sick, sad, or exhausted. We might also have some kind of meltdown. All of a sudden, we find ourselves crawling into bed to whimper like abandoned puppies or bursting into tears in public.

I am no stranger to both these kinds of meltdowns. If I trace back my steps, each crash was preceded by a clear decision to ignore my energy cycles. One particular meltdown stands out above all others.

During my yearlong odyssey of self-discovery, I spent a week in Auckland, New Zealand. While there, I joined forces with a group of friendly travelers. For two days in a row, I played the role of the hard-core tourist with my new friends. We explored, wandered, saw sights, and chased adventures. Every hour was saturated with new experiences. By the end of the second day I was utterly exhausted. I didn't have a single ounce of energy left for chitchat and social pleasantries. If I were to draw a diagram of my energy levels, they would have been in the red danger zone, about to self-destruct. Feeling drained and irritable, I began to withdraw into my inner world. However, despite my depletion, I decided to try to keep up with my new companions.

While en route from a local hookah bar to a dance club, one of the other travelers questioned my behavior. He pointed out that I wasn't talking to anyone and that I seemed to have put up an invisible wall. I tried to explain to him that I was an introvert. This was a big mistake. This man came from a highly extroverted culture where introverts are likely burned at the stake (okay, I'm exaggerating, but you get the idea). Introversion was a completely foreign concept to him. After a brief pause, accompanied by a look of disdain, he continued to press me about my behavior. Then it happened—without even the hope of stopping them, tears started streaming down my face. I began bawling my eyes out in front of this man, whom I hardly knew, while the rest of the group watched from about fifty feet ahead. I felt humiliated.

After sharing this story on my website, I received waves of comments from introverts with similar meltdown stories. We introverts can save ourselves a lot of heartache and embarrassment by understanding and honoring our energy cycles while socializing. From experience, most introverts can roughly estimate how much social steam we'll have for a specific event, and how long it will take for it to run out. For example, we might have noticed that we can only spend about an hour at a party before we begin to fade. We are like introverted Cinderellas; our energy turns to dust at a certain hour, except that our party persona might even expire long before the clock strikes midnight.

This can be frustrating for social introverts who want to connect with people, but who only have so much juice in our social batteries to work with. It also makes social obligations, such as networking events, especially stressful. Networking turns meet-and-greet into a competition, where everyone has an agenda. Desperate to make a good impression, attendees strive to say the right things to the right people. If we live in a world that expects us to be constantly switched on, networking events demand our highest voltage. While we may be able to keep up for a while, introverts will be drained more quickly at these events. This was the case for one of my introvert students, SuanPeng, a Korean concept artist trying to break into the entertainment industry. He explains:

> As an aspiring illustrator/concept artist in the entertainment industry, it is necessary to network and learn from those who have already made it there, as the bulk of the job relies on connections. Too many times, I would gather and chat for a while during

an artist meetup, but then after about half an hour, I just stopped being able to voice my thoughts anymore. I would just sit there quietly whimpering to myself, no longer engaged in their small talk and no longer laughing at their jokes. I felt so insecure and unsafe; like what if they just end up deciding to [cast] me [out]?

I want to be there for the good stuff—industry secrets and the exchange of knowledge and ideas. But I just don't have an energy tank filled [high] enough to sustain me through all the small talk. By the time they start talking about the industry, and I want to chip in, I feel awkward and disingenuous because I haven't been joining in their small talk.

I'm sure most introverts can relate to SuanPeng's story. I know I certainly can. Situations like these bring to mind the image of a surfer trying to ride a weak wave—he won't get very far. Likewise, introverts are slowed down by the low tides in our energy cycles. If we're not careful, we easily lose balance, or shut down altogether. Fortunately, understanding our energy cycles allows us to plan accordingly. If we have a big event on Wednesday, for example, we can schedule extra downtime later in the week. Likewise, if we know a party will outlast our energy supply, we can plan to leave early. Another option is for introverts to extend our social batteries. We can do so by 1) preparing ahead of time, and 2) choosing the right activities.

Preparing Ahead

The main reason introverts are drained by social activities is because those activities feel like a sensory assault. After a short period, we want to shut down and turn inward just to end the onslaught. Since we can only handle so much stimulation at a given time, reducing stimuli will extend our social batteries. There are many easy ways to decrease stimulation throughout the day. Just turning off the lights or closing our eyes for a while will work wonders. We can also reduce noise by turning off the television and spending some time in silence. Like adding quarters to a pinball machine, adding quiet to our day extends how long we can endure socializing. Many introverts are passionate music lovers who constantly play their favorite tunes in the background. Though music can be soothing, it is a form of stimulation nonetheless. Even if you like to have background noise most of the time, try steeping yourself in silence the hour before you go out.

Introverts feel best when we prioritize our energy when planning our social activities. One powerful exercise for getting started is to perform an energy audit. Here's how:

Make a list of all the activities that deplete you during a regular week. Then make a list of all the activities that replenish you. Once you have your two lists, rank each item on a scale from negative ten to positive ten, negative ten being the most depleting, and positive ten the most rejuvenating. Activities that neither fill nor drain your energy receive a zero.

If you add up the scores from all your weekly activities, are your energy levels in the negative? If so, start prioritizing the activities that give you energy, while avoiding energy vampires as much as possible.

Choose Wisely

A while ago, I read *Secrets of the Millionaire Mind* by T. Harv Eker. One of Eker's "wealth files" states, "Rich people think 'both.' Poor people think 'either/or.'" While I love this concept, and have since applied it in certain areas of my life, it's not always realistic for introverts, especially when it comes to socializing. Sometimes, introverts simply don't have the energy to do both. We must make a choice, and we must choose wisely.

If we only have the energy for one social activity on the weekend, the wise choice would be the option that provides the greatest payoff. This might seem straightforward, but sometimes it's tough to know what will be the most rewarding. Often, we have a hard enough time just deciding whether to leave the house or not. Like finicky cats, we hover at the front door, torn between home and the unknown. If we decide to go out, we inevitably want to come back in shortly thereafter. See if this sounds familiar:

You've been invited to a party by a couple of close friends. They have assured you that everyone attending is really "nice" and "friendly" and it will be lots of "fun." These words mean about as much to you as the squawks of exotic birds. You want measurable data. Exactly how many hours will you have to stay at this party? How many minutes of small talk will you have to endure? And how many times will you have to answer the same predictable get-to-know-you questions? It's also pertinent that you find out how many people will be there. Even more important is the ratio of strangers to familiar faces. Will there be any especially talkative and enthusiastic guests?

If you were to ask your friends all these questions, they would get annoyed. They would assume you are overthinking things or being a snob. They wouldn't understand that you are trying to calculate precisely how much energy this party will cost you. You're still a little hazy on the exact equation, but you know that people, noise, and flashing lights are all subtractions. You are well aware of how easy it would be to dip into the negative. This party will probably leave you in energy debt; however, there is a chance that it will be worthwhile. The payoff could justify the price. So, you stand in the land of indecision, a self-imposed purgatory between going out and staying in. Even the cat starts to roll his eyes at your indecisiveness.

Most introverts experience this sort of dilemma regularly. The decision of whether or not to go out is a difficult one because we know the rejuvenating benefits of staying home. Of course, leaving the house has its merits, too. We need love and connection in our lives just as much as extroverts do. True connection can be as replenishing as a night in for an introvert, especially if we've been alone for a while. That being said, a Friday night pub crawl probably won't provide many opportunities for the kind of connections that really fill an introvert up. That's why most introverts I know avoid the bar scene altogether. With this in mind, it might make sense to conserve our energy for smaller gatherings, where we can have more in-depth conversations.

We might also feel that an activity is worth what it costs us in energy if it supports our big-picture goals. We see the skills we build in a class or club as a good enough reason to go into energy debt. We happily endure the most dreaded networking event if it furthers our career goals. Even our career itself can be incredibly draining; yet, the sense of purpose we feel makes us willing to pay the high price in energy. This is the case for Gary, an introverted nurse who loves his job despite how draining it is:

> I am a nurse and I absolutely love my job; it is incredibly rewarding. But probably 90 percent of my coworkers are extremely extroverted, which can lead to some very lonely and exhausting shifts. I would certainly caution my fellow introverts against considering a career in health care, especially in a role like nursing, or practicing medicine for that fact alone. My one-on-one interactions with my patients are really what get me through the night.

For Gary, the payoff of working with patients is enough to keep him going despite his exhaustion. Other introverts in a similar situation might feel a career change is in order.

There is another reason the "choose both" mentality doesn't always work for introverts. Often, having too many choices is the reason for our mental exhaustion. Decisions are a major source of energy drain for introverts. This energy vampire is increasingly relevant as our culture focuses more on freedom of choice. Making decisions becomes more difficult as our choices expand. I'm not just talking about the big decisions, like where to live and who to marry. It's the smaller daily choices that have really gotten out of hand.

Gone are the days when we merely had to choose between black coffee and coffee with sugar and cream. Now we have to decide whether we want it medium, light, or dark roast; skim, 1 percent, or full fat; with or without foam. Just when we think we've got it all sorted out, they throw us a curveball, and ask "Would you like a shot of hazelnut?" *Damn. Hadn't thought of that, but it does sound good. Oh, but the calories* . . . Before we know it, we're having a mini-crisis over what kind of coffee to order. And we've still got a whole day of decisions ahead: what to wear, what to have for lunch, whether to spend lunch alone or be sociable, what to do after work, where to find the perfect gift for our mother-in-law.

We're starting to get used to this whole being a grownup thing, so the above decisions don't really faze us, but then we open up our laptops and are assaulted with a virtual buffet of choices that we didn't even know existed. Thanks, Google. Maybe it sounds like I'm exaggerating, but decisions really can be a serious source of mental exhaustion. This became clear to me a while ago while I was traveling through Thailand. Much of my time there was spent wandering the crowded streets in search of food. Constantly deciding when, where, and what to eat for my next meal was exhausting. Normally, picking a restaurant to eat at is fun. But when you're doing so three or four times a day it can feel overwhelming. This is because every decision we make takes mental energy. The hamster only has so much juice, so the more energy we sink into making choices, the less we have for other things.

This is why so many introverts (myself included) love routines. Routines and rituals eliminate choices. They put certain parts of our day on cruise control, allowing us to free up mental space for other more important things—like daydreaming. Reducing the amount of decisions we make in a day will help prevent us from being overwhelmed and exhausted. Beating the decision monster can be as simple as planning our daily lunches ahead of time. Putting a morning routine in place that doesn't require much thinking will also help. Since the Internet is a virtual Pandora's box of choices, it's a good idea to limit how much time we spend in cyberspace.

The People Who Drain Us

"People inspire you, or they drain you—pick them wisely."

—Hans F. Hansen

Just as some social situations are more draining than others, so are some people. This is why introverts are selective with whom we share our time and energy. Not just anyone will do. As Anaïs Nin put it, "I am lonely, yet not everybody will do. I don't know why, some people fill the gaps and others emphasize my loneliness."

Introverts must consider the energy exchange that occurs when making friends. We tend to invest more in each interaction than extroverts, and we want a greater return on our investments. We would rather experience a deep connection with one person rather than superficial pleasantries with several. Flitting from person to person at a gathering quickly drains us. Socializing in this way is all energy out and no energy in.

We're also influenced by how others use their energy. Some introverts feel best when we have an extroverted sidekick to nudge us out of our comfort zone. We appreciate the extrovert's high energy. Our extroverted friends are the sparks that ignite us. When our social stamina diminishes, extroverts take the reins, allowing us to go quiet and daydream for a while.

Of course, there are downsides to relying on extroverted enthusiasm to give us a jolt. I once dated an extroverted man whose energy was all-encompassing. It shot to the back wall and bounced off the ceiling of any room he entered. In small doses, he made me feel energized. I joked with him that I needed "a shot of Jared" to get me through the week. For me, he was the equivalent of three shots of espresso. The problem is, I'm hyper-sensitive to caffeine. Even half a cup of coffee makes me jittery. The inevitable crash is not worth the short spike in energy. It was much the same with Jared. Once we began spending heftier portions of time together, I became overwhelmed. It was as though I had reached my maximum energy intake and I was starting to short-circuit. I was irritable and overly sensitive, wired for meltdown. Just as some introverts can guzzle espresso with little effect, some would be able to handle Jared's intense energy in larger doses. Others would immediately be overwhelmed by it.

A lot of introverts feel most energized by personalities similar to our own. Such relationships leave room for comfortable silences, allowing us to recharge in tandem. Slower paced conversations mean that we can talk longer without feeling overwhelmed. We also better understand one another's needs. When one friend wanders off to recharge, the other does not take offense. Instead, she relishes the chance to do some refueling of her own.

Despite our energy challenges, we introverts can still do great things in the world. We really can feed the needy, or network like a champ. It all begins with working with the natural ebb and flow of our energy. In this way we can enjoy the hibernation periods in our energy cycle as much as the sunny peaks. Best of all, we won't have to worry so much about those dreaded meltdowns.

Just as a wheel needs an extra jolt of momentum to change directions, we may need to invest some extra time and thought into reshaping our life to suit our energy needs. Prioritizing our energy is well worth the investment. We are rewarded with the realization that energy is a renewable resource. We can refuel anytime we like.

4

Overcoming Mental Obstacles

"She's never where she is . . . she's only inside her head."

—*Janet Fitch*

We introverts love to wander. Our favorite destination for quiet explorations is our imagination. No matter where we are, we feel called away by our own thoughts. Anaïs Nin described the feeling well: "I'm restless. Things are calling me away. My hair is being pulled by the stars again." We grow restless in the here and now, so we let our imagination kidnap us for a while. We dim the front porch lights and go on a fantasy adventure. On the outside we look "zoned out." Inside, we are bursting with bright ideas and dreams.

It feels good to wander the deep forests of our imagination. Sometimes, it's a necessary coping mechanism. Going inside our head helps us avoid overstimulation. We might be in a crowded place, full of offensive sounds and odors. We zone out to escape the chaos. A more scientific way of explaining it is that the brains of introverts and extroverts have different levels of psychological arousal. Arousal refers to the state of being alert and ready to respond to stimuli. In the 1960s, psychologist Hans Eysenck proposed that extroverts have a higher level of arousal, causing them to seek out greater levels of stimulation to feel awake and at their best. This is why extroverts tend to be more social. They are also drawn to risk-taking activities, while introverts are more risk-averse and contemplative. Since introverts need less stimulation to feel engaged, we prefer low-key activities. Exploring our imagination often provides just the right amount of buzz for our brain. Another reason we go mind-wandering is because we are bored. Maybe, we're in the middle of a conversation that is about as exciting as watching snails race. So, we check out.

It's easy for introverts to live our whole life this way—half in the world, half out. In her famous book *Eat, Pray, Love*, Elizabeth Gilbert recalls the way a friend once described her introverted father. "Your father only has one foot on this earth. And really, really long legs . . ." I chuckled as I read this because it reminded me of my own introverted father. Then I (reluctantly) realized that I truly am my father's daughter. After all, I've done my fair share of "spacing out." My daydreaming seemed to peak in my teens. Nowadays, I still spend plenty of time in my head, but I try not to live there.

A 2013 study by Randy Buckner of Harvard University might explain why introverts love being inside our head so much. Buckner found evidence that introverts have more gray matter in our prefrontal cortex. Since this is the part of the brain associated with abstract thinking and decision-making, it makes sense that introverts like to think things through before acting. While our tendency toward deep contemplation is usually helpful, it can also be a hindrance.

Wired for Worry

Constantly being inside our head leads to overthinking. Sometimes it feels like our mind is wired for worry. Our brain latches on to a particular problem and overanalyzes it. When this happens, it is all too easy for negative thoughts and concerns to flood our mind. We begin to overthink, and even obsess. Our mind becomes a typhoon of swirling thoughts that threaten to flatten us into the ground. We ruminate over all the shoulds that cloud our today and the what-ifs that weigh heavily on our tomorrow. Before we know it, we're feeling guilty about something we did five years ago. Or fearful of what could happen five years from now.

Sometimes, I catch myself having entire conversations in my head with people I've barely said two words to in real life. This can be fun if the conversation is pleasant. Much of the time it is simply my brain's way of playing out possible negative outcomes. A while ago, I worried that I had deeply offended a friend of mine by showing up late for a date. When I arrived, she seemed annoyed and frustrated. For nearly a week I imagined conversations with her in which I defended my absentmindedness against her lecturing. Later, when I brought it up with her and apologized for offending her, she admitted that she hadn't been upset with me. She had simply been having a bad day. This interaction, and others like it, made me realize the fruitlessness of worry. Having imaginary arguments and focusing on worst-case scenarios is a waste of energy.

As we've already discussed in the last chapter, an introvert's energy is a precious commodity. Our habit of overthinking, combined with our tendency toward overstimulation, makes mental exhaustion a common problem for introverts. Usually, our brain is a whirring metropolis of thoughts and ideas. Unfortunately, it is all too easy for us to become overwhelmed by our own thoughts. Before we know it, our buzzing metropolis turns into a gray zombie land and we start to feel like the walking dead. This is when the critical little troll in our brain comes out to play. There is a particular scenario that used to really get the troll in my head going. It could happen anywhere, but let's just say I am at a bar.

I would go into the bar feeling pretty good about myself. I know bars aren't really my scene, but I am with my friends, and I have some liquid courage on hand. Then I would start to feel tired. As my energy plummets, everything around me picks up speed. More people show up. The music gets louder. All of a sudden, new people are sitting at *my* table with *my* friends. This is when it would begin.

No matter how much I will myself to "be cool," "chill out," and "have fun," my mind would not oblige. This would make me feel like the bad guy. After all, my friends had invited me out expecting me to join in their fun. No one likes a party pooper. But I can't help but sulk. Then my sulking turns to shame. Before I know it, I am comparing myself to the jovial extroverts at my table. The little troll in my mind points out how much better they are than me in every way. They are friendlier, prettier, more articulate, and more likeable. Then the troll turns his bony finger at me and asks, "Why would anyone like you? You're so boring and uncool. Everyone can tell you don't belong here. What's wrong with you?" The troll is most vicious when I am tired or outside my comfort zone. In some particular scenarios, I have both circumstances working against me. The troll is in the heyday of his cruelty.

The key to preventing situations like this is to rein in our unruly thoughts and give our mind a break. For those who tend to live inside our heads, this is not easy. Fortunately, there are ways to work with our brain instead of against it.

Training the Brain

The thing that trips us up when it comes to overthinking is the belief that our mind is our master, rather than the other way around. We forget that we always have a choice when it comes to our thoughts. It may feel like our mind has the reins and we absolutely must go wherever it leads us. But we really do have a choice.

Just as a horse can be trained, so can our mind. My friend, energy healer, and equine sport therapist, Alexa Linton, likens our thoughts to horses. There are plenty of horses galloping by at any given moment, but we decide whether or not we want to get on a particular horse and ride it. Some of us are determined to get on every horse, even if we know we'll be riding in circles. We don't have to ride every thought into the dark recesses of our obsessive mind. We don't even have to pay attention to any given thought.

Often, we're tempted not only to get on a passing thought but also to give it a carrot. We reward our most obnoxious thoughts by giving them space to roam. We let them claim too much territory in our precious mental landscapes. We also reward negative thoughts by giving them our focused attention. We ignore all the other beautiful horses in the barn and treat the most untamed, ugly beast of a horse as if he were king of the haystack. There is another option; we can let those wild, obnoxious thoughts—the ones we know will throw us and make us sore for days—trot on by. The less attention we give to such thoughts, the less they will pester us, and the more mental space we'll have for the other pretty horses we've been neglecting.

It takes practice to consciously choose constructive thoughts over destructive worries. If we've let our thoughts run wild for a long time, it can be especially hard to rein them in. The untamed mind is a chaotic and frightening place. Leave us alone with our mind for too long, and our angriest and saddest thoughts will band together to rob us of mental peace. "[Y]our mind is like an unsafe neighborhood; don't go there alone," explains Augusten Burroughs in *Dry*, his memoir about overcoming alcoholism. While therapy and coaching certainly makes braving the "unsafe neighborhood" in our head easier, it can only go so far. It's not like our therapist can actually climb inside our brain and evict all the bad guys. We can begin making the dangerous places in our mind safe again by choosing the right daily activities.

Finding Your Flow

Not all activities done in solitude are equal. Some rejuvenate us, while others make us feel more frazzled than before. Doing our taxes in silence, for example, probably won't leave us feeling particularly peaceful. Even activities we enjoy, like surfing the net or playing video games, can disturb our peace of mind. This is because electronic-based activities are more stimulating than other quiet pastimes. Bright screens and flashing images tire our mind. Sometimes, our brain self-sabotages while in solitude. No matter how soothing the environment, our mind will not shut up. It reminds us of chores we've let pile up and people we've let down.

Worries are less obtrusive when we choose activities that bring us into a state of flow. When we experience flow, we are completely immersed in what we are doing. We are so absorbed in the present moment that time falls away and we forget our worries. A friend of mine is obsessed with ice climbing. Climbing up a mountain in the bitter cold does not sound like much fun to me, but when she explained why she loves it, I immediately understood. "It forces me to focus only on climbing, because if I don't, I could fall. It's the only time I forget everything else—all my worries, my work, everything—and just focus on what is right in front of me." What my friend was describing was the sensation of being in flow.

A few years ago I took up sewing. I spent hours creating dresses and dance costumes. I was so absorbed in my creations that hours flew by without my noticing. Nowadays, I experience flow most when I'm writing. Instead of sewing fabric, I stitch together ideas. When I'm immersed in a writing project, I can't think about anything else. Writing gives me plenty of footholds to climb out of all the dark places my thoughts want to go. Other introverts might feel this way when they are playing the piano, gardening, or cooking. Anything that fully immerses us in the present moment will also give us respite from our worries.

Letting Go

Some thoughts are extra sticky. As much as we try to distract ourselves, these worries cling to us like leeches. A while ago, a student of mine, Jonathan, sent me a message about his struggle to let go of a particular problem. He explained, "I've been stuck on a problem for a long time and unfortunately it dominates my thinking and hinders my progress. It's stopping me from being present and being as happy as I could."

Like Jonathan, many introverts have a habit of lugging our problems around like last week's garbage. We insist on keeping the problem at the forefront of our mind where we look at it up close from every angle. We fold and unfold it. We pull it apart, then piece it back together. Finally, when all else fails, we put a giant sticky note on our prefrontal cortex, reminding us to revisit the problem again in a few hours. In other words, we are problem hoarders. No wonder our brain feels so cluttered.

Letting go means accepting that we can't work on a problem 24/7. Some things can't be fixed—at least not right away.

Whenever I used to encounter a technical problem with my website or business software, I would go in circles trying to fix things. Sometimes the issue was resolved quickly, but other times the solution evaded me. After snuggling up to a problem all night a few times, I realized that doing so was pointless. Technical problems become increasingly obnoxious as the night wears on. The more tired I was, the more impossible the problem became. After a good night's rest, a solution often showed up in the morning.

It's like this with nearly every brain bug that makes us worry late at night. Sometimes, we can't find a solution until we give our brain a break for a while. While our conscious mind is snoozing, our subconscious takes over and finds the answer. There is actually a term for this process of allowing the subconscious to solve problems. It's called the "incubation period," and it has long been recognized as an integral part of the creative process. We let our problem "incubate" while our subconscious whittles away at it, drawing upon thoughts that arose during conscious work.

The key thing to note is that we do spend some time consciously thinking about the problem. Then we let it go so that the invisible elves inside our subconscious can assemble our fragmented ideas into something that makes sense. I liken the whole process to a bird flying. When birds fly, they don't constantly flap their wings. Birds spend a significant amount of time gliding through the air, letting the wind support them until they need to start flapping their wings again. When working out a problem, it's okay to coast for a while and let the solutions come to us.

It's difficult to let go of something we're worried about. It feels like we're leaving the house with the oven on. At any moment, everything could burst into flames. We think if we release the death grip we have on our worries for one fraction of a second, disaster will certainly follow. Usually, this is far from the truth. Clarity comes when we make space for it. Letting go will make room for the right solutions show up.

Why So Serious?

Introverts are known for being on the serious side. People see our thoughtful grimaces and tell us to "lighten up." As much as I hate it when people say this, they do have a point. Overthinking makes us feel heavy. It's like we are physically wearing seven layers of self-doubt and a winter coat of worry. When we shed our useless thoughts, we feel lighter, as if spring has come and we can finally leave the house without a coat.

But lightening up is harder than it sounds, especially if our mind has wandered into dark territory. I'm reminded of a time when I was consumed with jealous thoughts. If you've ever experienced jealousy, you know how quickly toxic thoughts can proliferate and drown out the voice of reason. I had been walking in the woods near my house, wading deeper and deeper into the thick fog of jealousy. I had been here before. I was no stranger to the wasteland of negative cyclical thoughts brought on by jealousy. I had vowed never to return. And yet, here I was again, struggling to rein in my irrational worries. I knew I had to make a choice: let my thoughts spiral out of control, or set them free. I wanted to let go, but my mind already had a vice grip on my fearful thoughts. So, I asked the Man upstairs to help me regain control of my mind. Seconds later, a friend cycled by on a small bicycle. He was wearing a silly hat and an open smile that said it all: "Lighten up, Michaela."

I chuckled to myself as I realized how simple the solution to my negative thought spiral was. Being the overthinker I am, I expected the answer to be more complicated. I thought it would show up looking sullen and serious, like me. But it was just the opposite. It was soft and lighthearted. It was a familiar face riding by with a smile. Lightening up allowed me to enjoy a sunny walk in the very same woods that had been clouded gray with jealousy only moments before.

Sometimes, the only way to fight a negative thought is with a positive one. Let them duke it out and see who comes out on top. With practice, the thought that feels better will start winning. When I'm stuck in a state of worry, I think of a particular friend who always makes me laugh. I revisit a memory of us having a giggling fit. This never fails to make me smile. It is the kind of smile that reaches deep into my chest and warms my heart. It's impossible to obsessively worry when your heart is being bear hugged by loving thoughts. In his poem "My Worst Habit," the Persian poet Rumi writes:

> . . . There is a secret medicine
> given only to those who hurt so hard
> they can't hope.
> The hopers would feel slighted if they knew.
> Look as long as you can at the friend you love,
> no matter whether that friend is moving away from you
> or coming back toward you.

When all else fails, a funny cat video will usually do the trick. This might sound trite, but it's amazing how even a small dose of comedy can lift us out of the darkest dungeon of negative thoughts. Here are my favorite go-tos for lightening up with laughter:

- Any of American author Anne Lamott's largely biographical nonfiction books
- The hilarious articles on David Thorne's website, 27bslash6 .com (the article "Missing Missy" is one of my favorites)

- The website Hyperboleandahalf.com, which offers funny, illustrated stories from creator Allie Brosh's life
- *Sh*t My Dad Says* by Justin Halpern, a book containing all the ridiculous things the author's dad has said to him
- Reruns of the CBS TV series *How I Met Your Mother*, an American sitcom in which a father recounts to his children the series of events that led him to meet their mother

These are just a few of my personal favorites. I realize that not everyone will share my particular sense of humor. It's worth the effort to discover what authors, blogs, shows, and YouTube channels make you laugh. Many introverts never think to explore the realm of comedy, choosing instead to focus on more "productive" activities. But our mind needs a break sometimes. A little bit of comedy can be the equivalent of seven days in Saint-Tropez for an introvert's busy brain.

Isolation, Loneliness, and Obsession

Even though introverts need alone time, it doesn't mean we should live in isolation like hermits. When I spend too much time alone, my thoughts become obsessive. Either that, or I'll enter a kind of mental fog where thoughts are muddled and tinged with gloom. Try to have a conversation with me at this point and I probably won't make much sense. I'm told that this is how extroverts feel when they stay home too long. It's as if being disconnected from the world creates mental static. Everything becomes fuzzy. It might take a lot longer for introverts to get there, but we, too, begin to feel mentally drained when we spend too much time alone. The tricky part is knowing where to draw the line. How do we know when our sweet solitude has gone sour and it's time to emerge from our cave?

When loneliness creeps in, it is usually a sign that it's time for us to go out. For introverts, loneliness can be so stealthy in the way it sneaks up on us that we are surprised by its arrival. It is subtle at first and easily brushed off as a passing mood swing or a dip in blood sugar levels. Eventually, however, it becomes addictive. I know this seems counterintuitive, but humans are complex creatures. Introverts are as inscrutable as they come. So, after days or weeks of loneliness, we lose interest in going out and socializing. It all seems like a nuisance. We've settled into our isolation. Made a home of it. Unfortunately, our obsessive thoughts have settled in as well; the sofa has even taken their shape. Meanwhile, we are tiptoeing very close to the edge of insanity.

We can avoid isolation-induced insanity by planning ahead. Every introvert differs in how much time they can spend alone before loneliness takes hold. Some introverts can go for weeks without seeing another human and feel fine. Others thrive on the comfort of constant companionship from a trusted partner or friend. I'm starting to lean toward the latter. When I go more than a couple of days in a row without human interaction, I become restless. I start to feel agitated, morose, and self-critical. Now that I work from home, loneliness sets in more quickly. The important thing is to know what our needs are, and plan for them. If we know we can only handle two days without seeing people, make sure to schedule a date with a friend within that time frame.

Our mind can create a lot of chaos if we let it. Luckily, it is possible to house-train our brain by giving it the right toys to play with; a few pretty horses and a funny friend or two are a good start.

When we find ourselves struggling against negative thought spirals, we can lift ourselves out with a dose of humor. As we seek to master our mind, we mustn't overlook the importance of human connection. As much as we enjoy living alone inside our head, it's nice to have guests every so often.

5

Sidestepping Communication Conundrums

I rarely get to meet my introverted coaching clients in person, but when I do, I'm always surprised by how smoothly our conversations flow. You would think that a meeting of introverts would be stilted, punctuated by folded arms and awkward silences. Instead, we instantly connect over shared ideas and interests. We respect one another's speaking time, rarely interrupting or changing the subject too soon. The pace of the conversation is just right, allowing for thoughtful pauses and slow-moving sentences. I appreciate these kinds of conversations with fellow introverts because I know what the alternative is.

When talking to extroverts, things don't sync up quite so nicely. I know the reason is that introverts and extroverts communicate differently. Sometimes it feels like we aren't even speaking the same language. I'm reminded of the story of my Egyptian friend Moe's unexpected stint as a translator. One summer, Moe and our friend Julia went on vacation in his homeland. While there, Julia fell in love with an Egyptian man who did not speak a word of English. Since Julia did not speak Arabic, they asked Moe to translate their conversations. For the first year of their long-distance relationship, they would call

Moe late at night or in the middle of his exam period, begging him to translate their Skype arguments. Most of the time he begrudgingly obliged. Moe's sacrifice didn't go to waste. Julia and her Egyptian love got married a few years later. They can now argue to their heart's content without a translator. Much like Julia and her now-husband, introverts and extroverts need a translator to step in for a while to help us understand one another. Over the course of this chapter, I will be that person.

I assure you that I am fluent in introvert speak. I am all too familiar with the many challenges introverts face when conversing with extroverts. Though I still struggle with the communication issues we'll discuss, things felt a lot more dismal in my teens and early twenties. Back then, I didn't know that my slow-talking ways were an introvert thing. I had no idea that other people felt as awkward in group conversations as I did. Or that there was a whole segment of the population who couldn't stand talking on the phone. To my younger introverted self, I was simply defective. I kept trying to find the right button to press or wire to tweak to turn myself into a smooth-talking extrovert, but it never worked.

Instead, I got really good at being "the quiet one." I was the one who let everyone else do the talking, even if I knew I had something interesting to add to the conversation. Sometimes I tried to speak up, only to be interrupted. Or, I would say the perfect thing ten minutes too late. Group conversations were the worst because I never knew when to chime in or what to say. Listening to all those people made my mind go blank. The extroverts seemed to have no problem talking over one another, spitting out the first things that came to mind, but I couldn't figure out how they decided what was interesting enough to share. Much of the group dialogue seemed pointless and boring to me. So, I kept quiet. On the rare occasion I would build up the courage to say something brilliant (okay, probably not that brilliant), but no one heard me. Someone else would say the same thing five minutes later, and they would get all the glory.

One-on-one conversations usually went more smoothly, but they, too, had their challenges. If I was talking to someone who spoke quickly or interrupted a lot, I stammered or gave up mid-sentence, letting my words trail off like wounded slugs. "She's just going to interrupt you anyway, so why bother finishing your sentence?" my worn-out brain reasoned. Then, my sadistic mind would ditch me in the middle of my thought, leaving me to fumble for words.

With close friends, things flowed more naturally. This was partly because I felt more comfortable with old friends and family and partly because they actually listened to me. Still, after a while my mind would check out. I would lose footing in the conversation and slip into my own world of fantasy. I felt like Charlie Brown listening to his teacher—I saw people's mouths opening and closing, but all I heard was "wah waah wah wah waah." Like the other communication conundrums I've described, this still happens today, but to a lesser extent. I've trained my brain to stay present longer. I've built up my concentration muscle so I don't "zone out" nearly as much.

My communication struggles made me feel inadequate, to say the least. Words are wielded like scepters in our culture. He who holds the sacred talking stick has all the power. Smooth talkers—the ones with seamlessly flowing sentences and perfectly timed jokes—are the chosen ones. They win popularity contests. They get the girl, the job, and the glory. They are the ones introverts might look to as a standard to strive for, and we feel bad when we fall short.

Introverts don't need to become smooth-talking extroverts to connect in conversation. Once we understand our unique communication challenges, we can gently sidestep them with the quiet grace that is the essence of introverted charm.

Let's start by exploring some of the unique communication "introvertisms" we face.

Easing In

My brother and his wife have four kids. His wife also takes care of someone else's child a few times a week. After being dropped off, this two-year-old girl sits at the front door playing quietly with shoes for at least an hour. It takes her most of the day to warm up, but by mid-afternoon she is a different child. She giggles and runs around. Her face is more open and animated, and she also makes a lot more eye contact. Grown-up introverts need time to warm up to new people and environments, too. Even if we are confident and socially adept, we might feel inhibited when we first arrive. Our body, our words, and our facial muscles are stiff at the beginning. As time passes, we start to thaw out. We relax. Conversations feel less strained, as do our facial expressions.

New friendships require some easing into as well. An introvert will usually take longer to share personal information than an extrovert. Years could go by before we share things that others would divulge during a first conversation. Most of my close friends who read this will be nodding knowingly. It took me several years to tell one dear friend that I used to be married (I married at age twenty and divorced two and a half years later). "I didn't know that!" she said, eyebrows raised in surprise. "I'm working on my sharing," I said. It wasn't that I was trying to keep it from her; I simply hadn't thought to tell her. I suppose part of me was waiting to be asked about my past. That's the thing about introverts—we are always waiting to be invited to speak up about what matters to us. If the invitation comes too soon, we'll probably avoid the question, deflecting the focus to the other person. We might want to come closer, but we're not warmed up yet. We're still hanging out by the doorway, daydreaming in a sea of shoes.

Slow Is Not Stupid

Introverts tend to speak more slowly than extroverts; unfortunately, we live in an instant-coffee kind of culture that values speed. Everyone around us seems to have a hot-potato tongue and words that race like drunken rabbits—everyone, that is, except for the fellow introverts in the room. Unless we're talking about a topic that we're very knowledgeable or excited about, the words don't come easily. Our slow-talking ways have a lot to do with how our brains work. One of the reasons it takes us longer to verbalize our thoughts is that introverts rely on long-term memory more than working memory. Accessing the right words from long-term memory takes longer. This is why gathering our thoughts can feel like reaching into a pen of rambunctious bunny rabbits—there are so many bouncing around that it's hard to grab on to the one we want. By the time we do get a hold of the right thought to share, the conversation has already raced away from us. On top of that, the person we're talking with has made one of three assumptions about us:

a) We're not so bright.
b) We're not really interested in the conversation.
c) We don't want to talk, so it's okay to monopolize the conversation and interrupt us after even the slightest pause.

Usually, it's none of the above. In fact, assumption "c" is one of the most frustrating misconceptions introverts face. Just because we don't talk much doesn't mean we have nothing to say—quite the opposite. Give us a little time and encourage-ment and we can be quite the conversationalists. The confusion lies in the way that introverts approach conversation.

Extrovert conversations resemble a game of Ping-Pong with back-and-forth dialogue delivered at a dizzying speed. Introverts, on the other hand, prefer to take our time with each topic. We would rather dive deep into one subject than hurriedly skim through several. I equate it with the traveler who goes to Europe for a month and casually meanders through two or three countries versus the eager beaver who tries to cram in as many countries as possible. Introvert author Laurie Helgoe says that introvert conversations are like jazz: "Each player gets to solo for a nice stretch before the other player comes in and does his solo."

We shouldn't feel bad about our slow-talking ways. Speaking slowly is a key component of effective communica-tion. It allows others to understand, process, and appreciate what we are saying. It can also make us appear more confident because speaking quickly is a sign of nervousness. Taking time to compose our thoughts before speaking has the added advan-tage of making us appear more intelligent. Small pauses show that we are thinking. They also increase anticipation and ten-sion, drawing the listener in.

Sometimes, we desperately want to keep up with fast-talking extroverts. We would love to be able to fire off a quick and convincing answer on the spot. We fantasize about being the guy who always says the right thing at the right time, or the girl who can talk at length about any subject you throw at her. All of this sounds very appealing to us, but there is one prob-lem: our brain will not cooperate, and neither will our mouth, or the rest of our body for that matter. Though we might never talk as fast and furiously as our most extroverted friends, there are things that we can do to pick up the pace in conversation. If you want to think and talk fast during an interaction, it's a good idea to prepare ahead of time. Preparation could involve:

- Role-play exercises with a friend (this works well when getting ready for an interview)
- Reading up on current events
- Stalking people's Facebook profiles to find out their interests (oh, come on, we all do it)
- Exercising and getting enough sleep so your brain is fresh
- Coming up with some go-to responses, such as "that's interesting, tell me more about XYZ," or "I'm curious, what made you decide to do that?" One of my personal favorites is, "How did that feel?"
- Writing out want you want to say so the right words are fresh in your mind

Staying Silent

> "Silence is only frightening to people
> who are compulsively verbalizing."
>
> —*William S. Burroughs*

Sometimes, we're so tongue-tied that nothing comes out at all. In a world where even a short span of silence is deemed awkward, the pressure to speak up weighs heavily on quiet introverts. People want us to say something—anything—to fill the empty airspace. This is challenging for introverts for several reasons.

For one, we don't want to just say anything. Since introverts tend to listen more (though not necessarily better) than extroverts, we often find ourselves downstream from some

Chatty Cathy unloading every mundane detail of her life on us. The words flow out unfiltered. There is no thought as to whether what she is saying is interesting, important, or of any value at all. She simply verbalizes every experience and passing thought that is rattling around in her brain. This kind of oversharing does not appeal to us. Talking is so mentally draining that we would rather save our energy for topics that are meaningful. A lot of people forget that conversations are highly stimulating. For introverts, who are more easily overwhelmed by external stimuli, just listening to another person can be mentally exhausting. Add onto that the task of constant talking, and it's easy to see why introverts often opt to stay silent.

Another reason for our silence is that most introverts have been chastised for our tight-lipped ways. Extroverts love to point out how quiet we are. You've probably been asked, "Why are you so quiet?" several times in your life. And I bet it hasn't once made you want to launch into a soliloquy about why you don't talk much. Generally, introverts don't know how to respond when people point out our quietness. Umm . . . thanks? Yes, I know? Instead of encouraging us to speak up, their comments make us want to retract, shut down, and stay silent.

We might also choose to stay quiet because we don't want to sound arrogant. Introverts are easily misunderstood, and we don't want to add arrogance to the list of misconceptions about us. We imagine that if we voluntarily share what's on our mind, we will sound like that pompous guy from third period English class, the one who raised his hand at every chance and gave painfully long-winded explanations. So, we swing to the opposite end of the pendulum and hardly share anything at all.

A common introvert conversation tactic is to keep the focus on others. If we keep everything about them, we don't have to talk about ourselves. However, one of the easiest ways to overcome awkward silences is also to give ourselves permission to share our passions, ideas, and opinions. This might feel uncomfortable at first. Perhaps, we think the person won't be interested in what we have to say; however, true friends want to know what matters to us. They even want to know the supposedly dull stuff, like what we did on Friday night or how our vegetable garden is coming along. Pauses in conversation are a great chance to update our friends on our lives. No invitation needed.

Offensive Language

Many of us are used to extroverts talking closer, faster, louder, and more aggressively than we would prefer, and sometimes, we don't mind their forwardness. Other times, however, the person we're talking to speaks an extrovert dialect that is too extreme for us to relate to, and we might feel mildly offended by it. We all know that rare individual whom we find impossible to warm up to. Others might describe him as jovial, friendly, or gregarious, but to us he is heavy metal at our garden party, chalkboard nails across our brain. A man whom I sometimes bump into at my favorite coffee shop is like this.

This man—we'll call him Sergei—has the demeanor and conversation savvy of a bulldog. He stands too close, spitting out questions interrogation style. Not only does he invade my personal space, he acts like he owns it. Too familiar, too domineering. This is not a conversation; it is an attack. Sergei robs me of my energy without offering anything in return. His interactions with me steal away my time, solitude, and valuable attention. At least that is how it feels to me in the moment.

Sergei is just one example of how certain extroverted (or simply obnoxious) conversation styles can feel uncomfortable for introverts. They make us want to put up a wall, which then makes us feel guilty for being guarded. We feel especially bad if we know the other person has good intentions and is just being friendly or curious; however, there is something in the way they talk, question, or stand too close to us that makes us put up our protective armor.

Introverts want to converse in a way that feels good to us, a way that doesn't feel like an assault, a lobotomy, or a really long soliloquy delivered by a bad actor. That's why we don't usually burst onto the social scene, ready to mix and mingle with anyone who crosses our path. We prefer to tiptoe in and test the social waters. We go under the radar for a while so we can pick and choose whom to talk to.

We might make a wide circle around the person who is always talking. Unfortunately, quiet people are good targets for those who suffer from verbal diarrhea. We also try to avoid the chronic interrupters, who make it hard for us to refocus and remember what we had planned to say before being interrupted, and who are never good for the self-esteem.

The thing is, there are many kind, caring, and well-intentioned extroverts out there who simply can't help interrupting. For these extroverts, it's completely natural to interrupt and talk over other people. To them, interrupting to provide input, or their own personal story, is a way of moving the conversation forward. They also cut us off to show that they were listening by summarizing what we said. Can you see the irony?

Dealing with Chronic Interrupters

Imagine you are talking to an interrupting extrovert, who has just (surprise!) interrupted you. Instead of letting them hijack the conversation completely, you hold your ground. It might look something like this:

You: I'm really excited about—

Interrupter: The new season of *Scandal?* Me too! I've been thinking about it all summer and—

You: Actually, no. What I was saying was, I'm really excited about this illustration class I've been taking. The best part is—

Interrupter: That you get to draw nudes! I always wondered what that would be like.

You: Nope, let me tell you what the best part is. It's that I can actually use these illustrations on my blog.

Interrupter: That's great! How's the blog going by the way?

You: Well, actually, I wrote this post about—

Interrupter: You know I started a blog a couple of years ago, but only wrote like two posts, then gave up.

You: Hmm. As I was saying, I wrote this post about how introverts hate talking on the phone and it got over five thousand Facebook—

Interrupter: You're not an introvert are you? You don't, like, hate people, do you?

You: Yes, actually, I am an introvert. So, anyways, as I was saying—

In the scenario above, you keep coming back to what you were trying to say until the interrupter lets you finish your thought. As you can probably guess, this is exhausting. I only do it if I have the energy. Sometimes, I can't be bothered because I know that I'll never see the person again, or that what I was saying wasn't important to me anyway. Other times, I'll hold my ground to prove a point. I want the person to know that I don't like being interrupted. Hopefully, they'll get the point quickly because I don't have the energy to "train" chronic interrupters for months on end. Just as puppies must eventually learn to stop peeing on the carpet, interrupters must learn to stop cutting people off. It's just good manners.

Small Talk—an Introvert's Kryptonite

While we might be able to avoid interrupting extroverts, there is one communication conundrum we can't seem to escape: small talk. Whether you call it chitchat, banter, or chatter, small talk has the same troubling effect on introverts. It pushes us to the edges of a room. It is the reason we are reluctant to meet new people. It is one of those social pleasantries that is inherently unpleasant. Small talk, you see, is an introvert's kryptonite.

Our distaste for small talk might cause some people to think we are socially inept or snobby. They imagine us turning our noses up at something that goes to the core of our culture. They assume that we don't like chitchat because we don't like people. In reality, the opposite is true. We avoid small talk because we know it is the white bread of conversation. There are no real nutrients in it, just empty calories. Small talk is meant to be light and fun. It flees from depth and meaning. Personal questions are considered inappropriate. Likewise, any emotion besides being happy or neutral is discouraged. Consequently, authenticity dies on the vine. The truth is that small talk allows two people to have an entire conversation without really getting to know each other. There is no connection in superficial banter, and intimacy is out of the question.

Small talk can, however, provide a slippery surface on which to slide into deeper topics. It is one of those annoying hurdles we must cross to get to the good stuff. It can also help us network, make new friends, and make a good first impression. Here are some tips for turning small talk into interesting conversation:

- Use jump-off points to launch into more in-depth conversation. This involves picking up on a key point the other person says and using it as a springboard to take the conversation in a new, more interesting direction. This works best if the jump-off point is a topic you and/or your conversation partner seem passionate about. For example, say someone talks about how they recently bought netting to keep deer from eating the plants in their garden. You can choose the topic of deer or gardening as a jump-off point. Perhaps you're an avid gardener, or maybe you have a funny story involving a deer. This is your chance to guide the conversation in the direction of your choosing.
- Provide others with jump-off points by sharing about yourself. We've already discussed that this can be difficult for introverts. It's not in our nature to share without invitation. However, not sharing creates conversational dead ends. Give the person you're talking with something to work with by offering some clues about your interests, opinions, and beliefs. Share a story involving your favorite hobby. Talk about an idea you've been obsessing about. Share your perspectives on travel and art.
- Use a combination of thoughtful questions, statements, and observations. A lot of people make the mistake of asking too many questions. This can make others feel like they are being interrogated. Try mixing things up by sharing your own insights before asking more questions.
- Encourage rapport by showing appreciation for the person you are speaking with. You can do this by acknowledging

what they say with affirming statements, such as, "I can see where you're coming from," "I know exactly what you mean," or "that is a great way of putting it; I never thought of it that way." You can then share your own story or insight related to what they've shared.

- Get curious. You've probably noticed that it's way easier to make conversation when you're actually interested in a person. You can spark interest in any conversation by getting curious about a person's motivations, worldviews, and passions. You wonder what is beyond the surface and make efforts to find out. Your conversation partner will sense your sincerity, and they will feel comfortable opening up.
- Resist the temptation to judge. Just as others can sense when you are genuinely curious, they can also tell when you are judging them. Judgment puts up an invisible wall in a conversation. It makes both you and the person you're talking to reluctant to take the conversation to a deeper level.

Why We Avoid the Phone

Some time ago, while talking on Skype with one of my best friends, I realized that something was horribly wrong. The video option was turned off. And, as we all know, Skype without video is just a phone. Like most introverts, I detest talking on the phone. This begs the question: why do introverts hate the phone so much? After giving it some thought, I've come up with a few possibilities.

Let's begin with the ring. Whether your phone sings, buzzes, or plays a piano tune, a ringing telephone is annoying. The phone doesn't care that you are busy or deep in thought. It pays no mind to the fact that you really don't feel like talking right now. A ringing phone wants your attention—and it wants it *right now*! I once had a friend who often put his home phone in the fridge in order to avoid its intrusive squawking. Thankfully, cell phones can be set to silent or vibrate.

The incessant bark of a phone presents an inner debate for an introvert: To answer or not to answer? That is the question. Usually, we don't want to pick up. We might promise ourselves that we'll call back later. Later could be three days from now, or never. Another option is to commit a communication faux pas and send a text in response to their call. This might be considered rude. As a last resort, we may have to actually answer the phone. What ensues is something introverts dread—a conversation robbed of any visual or physical cues. This means that our nodding and subtle facial expressions are of no use. The other person can't see when we are pausing to think, process, or pet the dog. All they know is that there is silence on the other end, and it is awkward. Additionally, we can't see their facial expressions either. For introverts who rely heavily on observation skills, this is frustrating.

Nearly every other form of communication is preferable to talking on the phone—Skype, text message, email, snail mail, Morse code—all these trump the telephone. Thankfully, with the rise of online communication, it's easier for introverts to avoid dreaded phone conversations.

Opening Up Online

Introverts are especially enthusiastic online. This became obvious when the introvert revolution started gaining momentum and several introvert articles, memes, and YouTube videos went viral. One reason we love the Internet so much is that it gives us the chance to use a more introvert-friendly form of communication. Many introverts feel more comfortable expressing ourselves in writing. We are tight-lipped word economists in person; yet we are surprisingly candid online. We pour out our hearts on online forums, writing things we would rarely share face-to-face, especially not with complete strangers. The anonymity of the Internet elevates its appeal to introverts. We can slip into online conversations without any fanfare and exit just as seamlessly. This has advantages and disadvantages.

Some online relationships aren't meant to extend beyond cyberspace, and that's okay. Then there are people that we would like to get close to, but don't because we can't make it past the realm of emoticons and push notifications. If we are looking for real-life connections—the kind where we can share a plate of pasta or a walk through the park—some face-to-face conversation will be necessary.

Simply recognizing our communication challenges for what they are is liberating for introverts. We see that they are a natural consequence of being an introvert in an extrovert-dominated world. Rather than eradicating our silent moments, we're better off quieting our inner critic. Chastising ourselves only makes us more tense and tongue-tied. The next time you find yourself on the receiving end of a conversation assault, take a moment to have a little self-compassion. Remember that other introverts share your slow-talking tendencies, your hatred of small talk, and your disdain for the phone. One of the easiest ways to find us is by getting on your computer and spending some time online (my website, www. introvertspring. com, is a great place to start).

6

Rediscovering Your Emotions

A few years ago, I came to the realization that I had been pretty numb for a while. It's not that I was depressed or unhappy. I just didn't feel a whole lot of emotion in general. It was like I lived in the neutral zone of feelings where everything is just kind of beige and blah. This didn't seem right to me. Why didn't I feel things deeply? Where was the spark? Being the introspective introvert that I am, I decided this needed further exploration. What had caused this inner numbness? And how could I fix it?

What I've come to understand is that my numbness was actually closely tied to being introverted and highly sensitive. Emotions are incredibly overwhelming. If you're sensitive and inwardly focused, emotions can be downright scary. In order to cope in very extroverted environments, where we face constant energy drain and overstimulation, one of the first things we shut down is our own emotions.

We might also feel like our authentic emotions are shameful and need to be hidden. We live in a culture that views vulnerability as weakness. Only certain emotions are deemed appropriate, and the rest must be hidden from view and suppressed. Hide your emotions well enough and even you won't know how to find them.

Messy Emotions

> "It's all messy: The hair. The bed.
> The words. The heart. Life . . ."
>
> —*William Leal*

Sometimes the problem isn't that we feel too little. It's that introverts feel too much. We experience unexpected tidal waves of emotion. The frustrating part about these emotional swells is that they are unpredictable. We could be sailing through daily life, ticking all the boxes for health and well-being: we exercise, get plenty of sleep, and eat lots of green stuff. Then, without warning, we have what I like to call an "unruly squid moment." I came up with the term a few years ago after having an unpleasant experience involving a giant jar of seafood antipasto. My Italian friend got me hooked on the oily appetizer, which consists of baby squid, shrimp, peppers, and oil. It looks gross but tastes delicious. One day, a nearly full jar slipped out of my hands and shattered on my dark hardwood floors. A mess of shrimp and squid jiggled atop a massive puddle of oily brine. The tentacles. The oil. The overwhelming scent of seafood—it was all too much. There have been many times when I have felt just as shattered and overwhelmed by the unruly ways of my own emotions.

Emotions are hard to control and contain. This is why we often prefer to avoid them altogether. We keep our feelings on the back shelf where they won't make a mess. To us, they are just an inconvenience. We think nothing of ignoring and denying them. What purpose could these unpredictable little nuisances serve in our life?

Why Emotions Matter

Emotions are like the litmus paper of life. They provide valuable feedback on what is working in our life "experiments" and what isn't. If we don't like how a particular experiment feels, we don't have to repeat it. We can change a few variables and try again, or we can do something entirely different. It's easy to get lost when we ignore emotional feedback. Our emotions give us clues about our strengths, passions, and preferences. Avoiding them inevitably leads to wrong turns and detours that lead us to waste time in extrovert territory. We go left when we should have gone right. We choose partner A (the one with the good résumé) instead of partner B (the one who makes us feel alive). Then we wonder why our love life is flatlining. We ask, "Where is the spark?" Our emotions have tried to tell us, but we muzzled them too well. Now all we can make out is a muffled sense of longing.

If we suppress our emotions, there are sure to be signs in other areas of our life. One surprising area where emotions have an impact is in our level of motivation. I once did a coaching session with a young, introverted man who was struggling with motivation. Despite his intelligence and ambition, he could not will himself to complete projects. He was both baffled and frustrated by his apathy. He asked me how he could motivate himself. I could tell that he was expecting a tangible answer, like a No-Fail Blueprint for Getting Shit Done or a Three-Step Action Plan to Skyrocket Productivity. That's not what I gave him. "Has anything significant happened in your personal life since you started to feel stuck?" I asked, sensing that there might be a deeper issue at hand.

"Well, my brother did die a few months ago," he said, curling the end of the sentence up into a reluctant question mark. He hadn't even considered that the emotions he stuffed down after his brother's passing could be influencing his drive (and probably many other areas of his life). Emotions that aren't dealt with will find a way to be heard. They cling to our right calf like a toddler being dropped off at daycare. "Stop!" they say. "Pay attention to me! Listen to me!" Even if we shake off our pesky emotions for a while, they are sure to find other ways of getting our attention. This young man's emotions were on an all-out strike. They refused to go back to work until he acknowledged their needs.

Another way our emotions shout for our attention is through our sense of vitality. Feelings affect our energy levels. This is obvious when we think of the most traumatic times in our life. We've all been there. After a breakup, job loss, or death of a loved one, our emotions weigh us down. It's not just the heavy emotions, like sadness and fear, that drain us. Supposedly lighthearted emotions can be just as burdensome. Love leaves us with an emotional hangover so overwhelming it makes our head spin. Excitement is just as exhausting.

In the past, people believed that low energy was caused by purely physical factors. Now, more and more research is pointing toward emotions. According to psychotherapist Mira Kirshenbaum, author of *The Emotional Energy Factor*, only 30 percent of our total energy comes from physical sources. The other 70 percent is emotional. This is why we see frail-looking Mother Teresa types who can give and give despite their age or circumstances. Kirshenbaum points out that the most energetic people make efforts to replenish their emotional energy. For example, they allow themselves mourning time after a loss. They cry until there are no tears left, and then they move on. They also use laughter to make big problems smaller.

Feeling Connected

Remember when you were a kid and making friends was as easy as sitting on the same side of the circle? There are a lot of reasons why friendships form more quickly in childhood, for example proximity, less stress, and fewer fears about getting close. Another reason is that we are more emotionally transparent in our youth. Our emotions are little white lights that glow in the night. They draw people in with their warmth and beauty. As children, we don't feel the need to hide our light. Our masks are not yet fully formed. Instead of being polite and appropriate, we show our true feelings. We hang our emotional underwear out on the front lawn for everyone to see.

Even introverted children tend to be more emotionally transparent than the average adult. In my early twenties, I worked as an early childhood educator for kindergarten-aged children. One little boy, Sam, was an obvious introvert. Most of the time, he was quiet and expressionless, his face a blank slate that conveyed little about his mood and emotions. But when his best friend, Tim, was around, that all changed. Around Tim, Sam's excitement, frustration, sadness, and boredom were visible in his facial expressions and body language. He was equally animated when his father arrived to pick him up at the end of the day. True to his introverted nature, Sam only revealed his authentic feelings to his most trusted friends and family. There is nothing wrong with Sam's exclusive approach to connection. The problem occurs when we don't share our emotions with anyone. Our poker face becomes too convincing, and we forget how to show our true feelings.

Expression over Extroversion

Even if we manage to stop avoiding our emotions, there is still one more important step to climb. It's the scariest part of all—we must actually express our emotions.

This might not sound like a very introvert-friendly activity. We can't imagine having to go through life spraying our feelings everywhere, like a garden sprinkler. This is only the case if we buy into the idea that expression is the same as extroversion. It is not. This isn't about putting ourselves out there or being more outgoing. True expression is more of an unpeeling.

Whenever I go on a date, I imagine myself unzipping an invisible armor over my chest. I open my heart and let all expectations and judgments melt away. What is left is a sense of peace. It's reassuring to know that revealing the essence of my emotions is more important than wearing the perfect outfit or coming up with a bunch of smart-sounding questions to prevent awkward silences. This doesn't mean that I dive straight into my greatest fears and insecurities on a first date. That level of vulnerability wouldn't match the circumstances. Instead, I allow whoever I'm with to catch a glimpse of what I'm feeling in that moment. I let them see past the overcoat. I give them a peek at the French lace of my soul—and just a peek is often enough.

Sometimes, we can be so detached from our emotions that we forget what it feels like to express them. If this is the case, creative expression can become the impetus. This was the case for Andrew, an introverted client of mine. On the surface, Andrew seemed to be your typical man's man. He had a deep, booming voice and a brusque way of speaking. His social life largely consisted of going for beers with the boys. But he wanted more. He wanted real connection with people who could relate to his hidden inner world. The trouble was that the friends who were ready to understand and accept him for who he was couldn't find him because he kept his internal treasures well concealed. The men he usually hung out with would balk at Andrew's sensitivity, appreciation for poetry, and romantic ideals. The solution: reconnect with his creative passions. Creativity is a less intimidating form of emotional expression for introverts who feel uncomfortable sharing their feelings. Andrew revived his passion for songwriting and playing the guitar. He also began attending monthly poetry nights at a local café. The people he met wherever he followed his creative passions were similar to him—not the brusque, stoic exterior Andrew, but the softer, more artistic Andrew he usually kept hidden. Expressing himself through art helped Andrew to connect with people in a deeper, more authentic way.

Of course, we can do artistic things without expressing any feeling, just like we can make food without any seasoning or have sex without being in love. Approaching art in this way is not satisfying for us, or our audience. When it comes to singing, dancing, drawing, painting, poetry, and any other form of creative expression, emotions matter. They can mean the difference between being "nice" and "good" (read, "forgettable"), and being captivating.

In my youth, I loved to sing. Much to my delight and terror, I was given a short solo in "Song for the Mira," which my high school choir performed at a handful of events. Whenever it came time for my solo, my heart picked up pace and my knees shook. My mind replayed all the instructions from my vocal teacher: *Stand up straight. Breathe through your diaphragm.*

Project! During our final performance, I decided to drop the inner dialogue and just sing with feeling. Afterward, my good friend Moe exclaimed, "That was the best I've ever heard you sing!" I knew it was the emotion behind my singing that made the difference.

Finding Your Feelings

No matter how we choose to express our emotions, we will have to find the damn things first. This is challenging for introverts who've trained ourselves to ignore and detach ourselves from our emotions. It's as if we are fumbling our way through the darkness, feeling around for things we've never felt before. We don't know their consistency, texture, or weight. We only know what these emotions look like on the outside. This can be very different from how they feel on the inside.

Parenting is a perfect example of this. When those of us without children look at the tired, ragged exterior of parenthood, we wonder why anyone would voluntarily subject themselves to such torture. We can't fully understand the appeal of having children because we don't have all the data. However, if we were to climb inside the emotional core of parenthood, we'd have a completely different perspective. We would feel the love, the fullness, and the compassion. We might feel some not-so-shiny emotions too, like frustration, boredom, and anger. But I'm guessing the love would win out over even the whiniest, snottiest, most vomit-covered emotions. Or at least, I hope so.

There are three ways that we can make identifying our emotions easier. 1) We can use a flashlight to search for a specific emotion. 2) We can turn on the lights. 3) We can enlist the help of others.

The Flashlight Method

Darkness has its appeal. It lets us disappear into the blackness and feel invisible. Turning on the lights means we actually have to look at ourselves—sometimes, for the first time in our lives. Many of us would rather get out a flashlight and hunt for a specific emotion. "Where did my bliss go?" we wonder, wagging our flashlight to and fro like a dog's tail. "And what did I do with my anger toward my father? I could've sworn I saw it a minute ago." Though we might find what we're looking for using the flashlight method, it will take longer than just flicking a switch.

Turning on the Light

When we turn on the light, things that seem unrelated come into focus. We see that our current sadness is connected to our past feelings of rejection. We are suddenly aware of the link between our introversion and our nagging sense of guilt. No wonder many introverts describe discovering their introversion as a "lightbulb moment." Illuminating our introversion brings us face to face with feelings we brushed off and told to get lost. This sudden awareness of our personality, and all the resultant behaviors and emotions, vindicates us.

Turning on the light is all about bringing awareness to what's going on inside our heads, our hearts, our souls, and even our guts. It helps us to view all of these aspects of self as being connected. When we think a thought, we can ask ourselves how that thought makes us feel. When we feel an emotion, we can ponder what thought preceded that emotion. Then we can check in with our gut and see what it has to say on the matter. Where the flashlight method isolates, the light switch method integrates.

Enlisting Others

When someone goes missing, a search party is assembled. The more people there are on the lookout, the more likely the child will be found. It is the same with missing emotions. We can enlist the help of others to identify and reconnect with our emotions that have gone MIA. Many introverts are reluctant about taking this approach. We pride ourselves on being able to handle everything on our own. We have enough trouble asking our waiter if he can "please bring some ketchup if he's not too busy; really, no rush, and sorry for the trouble." Asking for emotional support of any kind is just too extreme. Surely we can figure out our feelings on our own.

The trouble is that our brain needs outside sources to offer insight. Otherwise, our well-worn thought patterns lead to dead ends. Books, online resources, and TV and radio experts can help. But reruns of *Oprah* and *Dr. Phil* can only do so much; nothing can replace the insight of a close friend or family member. Often, it doesn't even matter if the person we talk to offers any good advice. Simply talking it through with a real, live human being gives us fresh perspective. Friends who are genuinely empathetic are the most helpful. They understand our feelings when we don't. Sometimes, they can help us label our emotions. "That must feel so frustrating," they say with sincere compassion. Or, they share how they felt in a similar situation. "When I started my business, I felt totally inadequate. Even when things were going well, I felt like a fraud." Their words are both illuminating and validating.

The darkest rooms in our mansion of emotions are best visited with a professional. We need someone who has the patience to guide us around the sharp edges and the slippery parts that threaten to bring us down. A professional will know how to gently bring suppressed emotions to the surface where they can be labeled and released. A counselor, therapist, life coach, or spiritual teacher are all possible options.

Living with More Emotion

Often, we believe that there are only two ways to approach the daunting waters of our own emotions: dive headfirst into the recesses of our psyche where childhood traumas and pimply teenage rejections are anchored, or stay in the shallow end where we only explore happy, good, and politically correct emotions. But there is another option that works better for introverts.

We can start small. This is not the same as staying shallow. We ease into the realm of emotions by identifying the quieter kinds of feelings, the ones that don't feel quite so much like a punch in the face. These emotions might be closer to the surface, but that doesn't necessarily mean they are superficial. They still provide connection points for others to latch on. They also give us clues that point us in the direction of our most ideal, fulfilling life. Awkwardness, confusion, deflated, loneliness, curiosity, hopefulness, rebelliousness—these are all feelings that can make ripples in our daily waters. If we don't pay attention, they will pass by unnoticed, taking the messages they carry along with them.

Reconnecting with our emotions is as simple as naming one feeling we feel during the day. We might have experienced fifty, but identifying just one is enough. Perhaps, we felt inadequate at work, awkward at a social gathering, or vulnerable during a conversation with our partner. I know this might sound trite, but sometimes it's easier to describe our emotions with colors, textures, or analogies. Here are some examples:

- I feel warm and fuzzy.
- I feel fragile.
- I feel blue.
- I feel bubbly.
- I feel like a pressure cooker about to explode.
- I feel like there is a gray cloud hanging over me.
- I feel sparkly, like fireworks on New Year's Eve.
- I feel fragmented, like I'm in pieces.

A friend of mine recommends naming difficult emotions after people you know. For example, naming your anger after an aggressive uncle. Jealousy is given the same name as a possessive friend from college. The idea is that you acknowledge your most feared emotions, while at the same separating yourself from them. "Oh, there's Uncle Peter again," you say, as a wave of anger starts coming on. When jealousy shows up, you say, "Ah, Annie has stopped by for another visit." Identifying an emotion in this way helps you remember that it is a temporary guest that can leave just as quickly as it arrived.

No matter how we choose to reacquaint ourselves with our emotions, it's important to recognize that they truly are the undercurrent of life. While waxing philosophical with a fellow traveler a while ago, we talked about how emotions are essential to a full life. He said that one of the greatest lessons he learned from his many adventures abroad was that all emotions, even the painful ones, are valuable. He believed that both extreme happiness and sadness were equal in their importance. Both teach us about ourselves. Both make us feel alive.

The lowest emotional points of my travels showed me my true values. Loneliness and emptiness told me that true connection mattered more to me than many of my lofty goals. Anger and frustration let me know that I had taken a wrong turn. No matter how painful or frightening the emotion, it always reminds me that I am in the thick of this confusing, miraculous, outrageous, unpredictable mess that is life. I am alive, and that's gotta count for something

When we deny and suppress our emotions, our lives become stagnant and predictable. It's as though we are choosing to live in an IKEA showroom instead of a real home that glows and sings and creaks in all the right places. I've lived in a lot of homes over the years. One of my favorites by far was an old Queenslander (Australians will know what I mean) with creaky floors and screenless windows. I hated the mosquitos and cockroaches that inevitably crept in at night, but I loved the home's moodiness. It cackled with the rain, swayed with the wind, and beamed brightly on every sunny day. It was the perfect home in all manner of messy emotions—and tidy ones, too. So, if you want to reignite the spark of life, open the windows of your heart and let it all in: The sun. The rain. The joy. The cockroaches. Love. Life.

7

Taking a Turn toward Self-Love

"This is my simple religion. There is no need for temples; no need for complicated philosophy. Our own brain, our own heart is our temple; the philosophy is kindness."

—*His Holiness the Fourteenth Dalai Lama*

Like so many other aspects of an introvert's life, self-love begins on the inside. With this in mind, it makes sense to view our internal landscapes as sacred grounds. We are our own temple. For many of us, temples are mysterious structures that we might never enter. But even with our limited experience with temples, we know a few of their key characteristics. On temple grounds, there is quiet reverence. Purity is revered, while blasphemy is forbidden. After all, temples are meant to be home to the Divine.

Though we might never set foot inside a traditional temple, we are certain to erect one of our own making at some point in our life. Our temple is the place where we feel most connected to our power source. For a bodybuilder, the gym is the sacred structure where he feels most powerful. For an artist, her studio is her temple. Many of us construct temples within our workplace, or at least we try to. Some of us try to create a sanctuary within another human being (yes, even introverts do this). Yet, few of us honor the temple that is within. This is unfortunate because the same customs that keep a temple pure and peaceful will keep us in a self-loving state. Let's take a look at six temple practices that serve as shortcuts to self-love for introverts.

Prioritizing Purity

Temples are kept pristinely clean. You would never see a temple's interior walls covered with graffiti. Usually, there is barely a dust particle in sight. However, introverts tend to defame our interior world with all sorts of nasty judgments. We are the punk kids with spray cans, eager to vandalize our mind with bold criticisms. We are all too willing to do serious damage to our self-esteem. If someone were to ask us why we would spoil such a beautiful space, we might shrug our shoulders. "Is this place important or something? Looks pretty lame to me." This is the attitude we have about our rich inner world, our labyrinth of ideas and dreams. We think none of it matters; it's all worthless.

This is obviously not a self-loving attitude, but many of us are so used to seeing ourselves in this way that we don't know how to stop. Vandalism is addictive. Disfiguring something important makes us feel powerful, even if it is only ourselves that we are harming. In order to reclaim our sacred interiors, we must put down the spray can. We must make some nonnegotiable rules about the ornaments with which we choose to adorn our temple walls. What is fitting of such a sacred space? What is not? Our interiors may be in need of a serious spring cleaning.

If this is the case for you, here are a couple of questions to help you get started:

- How do you "vandalize" your mind? In other words, what criticisms or nasty comments do you say to yourself on a regular basis?
- What would happen if you put down the spray can and never said an unkind word to yourself again?

The words we throw into the air have a way of coming back to us. Harsh words tear through us, leaving our self-esteem in tatters. Kind, compassionate, and uplifting words put us back together again. Maya Angelou described words as living things. "They get on the walls. They get in your wallpaper. They get in your rugs, in your upholstery, and your clothes, and finally in to you." Words most definitely matter. For quiet introverts, the words we say to ourselves are even more important than those we share with others. After all, an introvert thinks more than they speak. Since our self-talk sinks into the wallpaper and upholstery of our inner temple, we had best choose what we say carefully.

My friend and colleague, Patricia Weber, author of *Communication Toolkit for Introverts*, advises that introverts speak to themselves in the second or third person. This makes sense, considering that we are much less likely to say hurtful words to others than to ourselves. There is scientific evidence to support the use of third-person self-talk. In a 2014 study published in the *Journal of Personality and Social Psychology*, psychologist Ethan Kross and a research team studied how people use different styles of self-talk during stressful tasks, such as delivering a speech. To summarize, people who used non-first-person self-talk were more at ease while delivering their speeches than those who spoke to themselves in first-person. They were also more likely to use positive messages, building themselves up just like they would a close friend or colleague. Members of the first-person group, on the other hand, were much harder on themselves.

Learning about the benefits of non-first-person self-talk instantly resonated with me. Over the past couple of years, I've been gradually shifting my internal dialogue. I realized that I had already been using third-person self-talk and can attest to its effectiveness. This might sound cheesy, but sometimes when I'm in a stressful situation I'll refer to myself as "honey" or "sweetie." "You're doing great, sweetie," I'll say. Or, I'll offer myself some words of comfort: "Don't worry, honey, it's all going to be just fine." Somehow, these sentences sink in more easily than if I were to say the same thing in first person. As much as we introverts hate to admit it, we do crave external validation, even if the "external source" is really just us speaking to ourselves in the third person.

Experiencing Inner Alchemy

A temple's interiors are often ornamented with gold and silver. We can all appreciate the beauty of precious metals in their gleaming final state, but few of us consider the process it took to make them shine. The medieval science of alchemy was based on the idea that base metals could be turned to gold through a seemingly magical process of transformation. When introverts fully embrace who we are, we undergo a kind of inner alchemy. We transform what society labels as negative traits into our greatest assets. Rather than trying to fix or cure our quieter qualities, we cultivate them. To do this, we must come face to face with our shadow self.

Our shadow self is comprised of all the aspects of our personality that we've been hiding. We hide these parts because someone told us they were shameful, inappropriate, or "not nice."

For introverts, this can mean hiding our innate need for alone time and any other aspect of ourselves that might be considered strange or rude. Even our gifts of introspection, deep thought, and imagination might be cast aside and deemed unacceptable. We hinge self-acceptance on our ability to fit into a narrow definition of normal. Any part of our personality that seems different gets stomped down and tossed aside, exiled indefinitely to the dark realm of shadows.

In his book *A Little Book on the Human Shadow*, Robert Bly describes our shadows as unacceptable qualities that we've thrown over our shoulder into a bag. Each quality we add to the bag increases the weight that we must drag along with us. It's natural to have a few shadows in our sack, but many introverts have stuffed the better part of our personality into the bag. It's not long before we start to feel weighed down by all our hidden parts.

When we accept and integrate our shadows, they add dimension to our personality. On the other hand, when we cut away our shadows, what remains seems manufactured and superficial. Our beautifully complex personality is sanitized, simplified, and crammed into a box. Any decent artist will tell you that shadows add depth. A lack of shadows creates a flat and two-dimensional picture. When we take the time to look into our bag of shadows, something magical happens. We begin to see ourselves for who we really are. We start to understand that we weren't born to be perfect. Our greatest qualities are tethered to our most feared flaws.

This inner alchemy process creates a kind of self-love that is unconditional. It is not hinged on our ability to be perfect. Rather, it thrives on the hope that we can be whole human beings. A great way to ignite the process is simply to be curious about our shadows. The most transformational questions begin with "what if":

- What if my sensitivity was my most loveable quality? How would that feel?
- What if my introversion is the key to my success? What would that look like?
- What if my love of solitude is what will allow me to connect deeply with others—maybe even my soul mate? What would I do differently?

By taking this approach, we develop a lighthearted attitude toward transformation. We ease into the promising realm of "what if." This is different than, say, trying to hammer a bunch of self-love affirmations into our head. Affirmations only work if we believe what we are saying. Asking "what if" allows us to simultaneously dance with doubt and possibility.

Finding Sanctuary

Holy places, such as temples, are known for offering asylum to the persecuted. In ancient Greece, for example, certain temples provided protection for ill-treated slaves. In the temple, fugitive slaves could find refuge from a life of abuse. During times of war, Greek temples of asylum were filled with deserters. The fleeing soldiers knew temple grounds would provide a safe haven from the chaos and conflict of war. Likewise, our inner landscapes are meant to be a war-free zone. A peaceful heart and mind provides fertile ground to cultivate self-love.

Many of us are constantly at war with our true nature. You've probably heard the saying that we are our own worst critics. For introverts, it can be a little more extreme than that. It's as if we are our own firing squad determined to shoot down every hint of a flaw in sight. I've never shot a real gun before, but I hear the kickback can knock you right over. Self-criticism is like this. If the shot doesn't take us out, all the energy wasted on pulling the trigger will. We have so many supposed flaws to shoot down that we don't know where to begin. We zero in on our low energy, chastising ourselves for not being able to bounce around from task to task as many extroverts do. Then we aim our anger at our sensitivity. Like tough-love Nurse Ratched, we think we can scold ourselves into toughening up.

In our war against ourselves, we employ nearly every tactic imaginable. But there is one strategy we overlook. It's the one simple act that has the power to save us, redeem us, and put our broken pieces together again: surrender. There is a saying in the self-development world: "That which you resist persists." It means that the more we try to fight an aspect of ourselves, the more persistent it becomes. For a long time, I resisted the more sensitive and emotional side of my personality. I thought these traits made me weak. However, no matter how hard I tried to contain my feelings, they would eventually emerge—and never in the delicate, controlled way I commanded them to. Like a hyperactive child who has been sitting for too long, my feelings became unruly and unpredictable. My constant battle against my own emotions made inner peace impossible. I didn't realize I could raise the white flag in the war against myself and surrender to my sensitivity and everything that comes with it.

The tricky part is knowing how to surrender. Whenever I feel tempted to go to battle with my own flaws, I remember all the loving words of advice I share with my subscribers and students. I speak gently to myself as I would a small child. I shift my focus toward my strengths. I take a nap. Often, settling into our own imperfections is the most loving thing we can do for ourselves. Some might equate surrendering to our flaws to sleeping with the enemy. I prefer to think of it as catching some shut-eye in neutral territory. After years of being in a war zone, taking a catnap in Switzerland is just what introverts need.

Focusing on Virtues

On temple grounds, visitors are invited to shift their focus away from the mundane and toward the world of deity and virtue. In Hindu temples, for example, the four important principles of human life serve as focal points. An elaborate network of art and carvings celebrate *artha* (prosperity), *kama* (pleasure), *dharma* (virtues), and *moksha* (self-knowledge). By highlighting the key elements of life, Hindu temples make it easy for visitors to focus and reflect on these principles. Part of developing a self-loving attitude is selecting worthy focal points for our inner temple.

Introverts have trained our brain to focus on our supposed shortcomings. Shifting focus is like shining a spotlight on our strengths. In my online courses for introverts, I always include exercises for creating major mind-set shifts. In one of these exercises, I ask students to list everything they "could be proud of if they were to be proud of something." Phrasing the question in this way helps students to move past their initial belief that they have nothing to be proud of. Once they shift their focus, they begin noticing their strengths.

After sending out the exercise, I often hear responses similar to Stefanie's, a student of mine: "I couldn't answer straight away in which areas of my life I felt most self-assured. And this is probably because I am not used to believing I am good at something. At all. It took me some days to remember what friends, family, and colleagues admire or praise about me." After giving it more thought, Stefanie realized that she had many things to be proud of. "I am actually proud of what I have achieved on my own! I speak five languages, I have traveled a lot, and I have a good job and good friends. I am independent and flexible. I am very capable of many things. [I am] more and more assertive and true to myself."

As we can see from Stefanie's experience, shifting our focus takes practice. There are plenty of us who have spent several years giving all our attention to where we lack, while ignoring our successes. It's true that not all introverts are timid, but we certainly shy away from our own greatness. I'm reminded of one of my favorite quotes by Marianne Williamson: "Our deepest fear is not that we are inadequate. Our deepest fear is that we are powerful beyond measure. It is our light, not our darkness, that most frightens us. We ask ourselves, 'Who am I to be brilliant, gorgeous, talented, fabulous?' Actually, who are you not to be?"

There is comfort in certainty. For a long time, we introverts have been certain of our inadequacies and frightened of our strengths. When we swap things around and become less sure of our shortcomings, self-love is the natural next step.

Filling Your Cup

The spacious solitude of the temple is the perfect atmosphere to fill our cup. It is the place to go to receive inspiration and rejuvenation from the Divine. For depleted introverts, the ability to receive can mean the difference between self-loathing and self-love. Distant deities are not the only ones with the power to replenish us. Learning to receive support from our friends, family, and community is just as nourishing for introverts whose cups runneth empty.

It's not just our energy levels that need replenishing. In his book *The 5 Love Languages*, Gary D. Chapman talks about the importance of keeping our "love tanks" filled. When we are loved in a way that we can understand, we are able to fully receive and reciprocate that love. This creates a dilemma for introverts who don't have the kind of fulfilling relationships we crave and need. We are emotionally depleted, and yet we feel guilty for not being loving and generous enough. We think we should be able to draw rose scented water from an empty well, but it doesn't work that way. If we expect to give our best to the world, we must learn how to receive.

Even if we don't have the close relationships we desire, we can still receive love and support. We've already discussed the importance of giving ourselves praise. Receiving kind words and acts of service from others is just as crucial. Have you ever noticed that the people who receive gifts with the most enthusiasm are inevitably given more gifts? That's why most of us love giving presents to children. We love seeing their eyes light up. They don't push the gift away and say, "No, I couldn't possibly," or "It's too much." They grasp the present with their tiny hands and receive it with delight. I have a friend who loves to give and receive beautiful gifts. I enjoy buying things for her because I know she will appreciate it. Her eyes will sparkle like a child's and she will say "thank you" as much with her facial expression as her words. In contrast, when someone turns down a gift or an offer of service, I feel little motivation to try again. After all, giving is an exercise in vulnerability. It opens us up to rejection. When people don't want our gifts, it feels as though they are saying they don't want us.

This is a tough concept for independent introverts to wrap our mind around. We think that receiving from others inconveniences them, and sometimes it does. But more often than not, it creates a point of connection between giver and receiver, and both parties are filled up by the exchange. Receiving from others can be as simple as saying "yes" when a friend offers to help us prepare or pay for a meal. Constantly saying "no" to offers of assistance ensures that no one will want to help us. Whenever I hear a woman complaining about her spouse not helping enough with household chores, I wonder how many times she had turned down subtle offers of assistance early on in the relationship. When her partner offered to help, she might have brushed him off, saying, "Oh, don't worry about it. I can do it quicker myself." After a while, her partner believed her and stopped offering assistance. Though doing it all on our own might seem easier at first, over time it wears us down.

Another reason we are reluctant to receive from others is that we believe we will owe them. We imagine that everyone is keeping an invisible scorecard, and we must keep the points even at all times. Of course, give-and-take is important. But in the moment, the most generous thing we can do for the giver is to say a sincere thank-you.

When it comes to filling our own love tanks, we must be both giver and receiver. Even for the most generous of introverts, giving to ourselves can be difficult. It might feel self-indulgent at first. Perhaps, we don't know what kind of gifts to give ourselves. We are like orphan children who've never been offered nice things. We have always just accepted the hand-me-downs—the scraps of what others have left over. We give the best of ourselves to others: our mental energy, our time, our good china, our kindest words. Meanwhile, we scrape by on fumes, barely harnessing enough energy to open a box of cereal. Filling our own love tanks means saving some of the good stuff for us. This will be different for each person. For me, the "good stuff" is a life-size loot bag of nourishing food cooked slowly just for me; time in nature, where my mind is free to wander and dream; a long soak in the tub while listening to Adele; writing in my pajamas; sleep.

Notice none of the things I mentioned were extravagant or expensive. Yet, for a lot of introverts they seem too decadent to accept. "I don't have time for that," we say. Meanwhile, we don't hesitate to give our time, money, and energies to our employers, accountants, spouses, and children. "But I have to work, and I must pay my taxes, and, of course, I have to take care of my children!" we say. If only we could feel as much of an obligation to ourselves as we do to our employers and families. I know it seems counterintuitive to even say this, but what if our own well-being was as important to us as that of our children? That doesn't mean we neglect the little ones in our lives. We can love those around us while also loving ourselves. Likewise, we can give ourselves gifts and receive them graciously without guilt.

Self-Loving Rituals

In the temple, rituals are conducted as symbolic actions that represent a passage or change. For introverts, rituals provide sacred grounds for self-love to take root. Many of us have

mixed feelings about the word "ritual." We imagine animal sac-
rifices and naked fire dancing. But a ritual can be as simple
as sitting in silence for five minutes in the morning. It can be
as sparsely luxurious as sipping hot lemon water and staring
into space. What turns these everyday activities into a ritual is
intention and repetition. The intention of a quiet ritual might
be to relax and refuel. Or it might be a way of reconnecting
with our intuition—a sort of daily check-in with ourselves. The
repetitive aspect of rituals ensures that they make their mark on
our lives. However short and simplistic the ritual, when done
daily, it becomes a part of who we are.

When I was little, my brothers and I spent every other
weekend at my dad's house. After he picked us up on Friday
evening, we would always stop by the corner store near his
apartment. We were each allowed to choose one treat. This
was the routine, our ritual. We had other simple rituals at
Dad's house. In the morning, he always cooked us a break-
fast of eggs and wieners or fish sticks. On Sunday evenings
we gathered around his little black TV and watched *Road to
Avonlea* (a Canadian family show set in the 1900s). Somehow, the repetition of these weekend rituals reinforced their
intention. My father may be a soft-spoken man of few words,
but his actions spoke loud and clear. Scrambled eggs and fish
sticks said "I care," while our predictable trips to the corner
store translated into "I love you." That's how it can be with
our daily rituals. Simple actions done with loving intentions
translate into self-love. Consistency ensures that the message
really sets in.

Self-love might feel unnatural after years of self-loathing.
Our inner temple is graffitied and full of insults toward
ourselves. We find it hard to feel at peace when we have been at

war with ourselves for so long. Self-love is the most important bridge we cross on the journey toward our true nature. Our authentic self cannot be seen through the lens of self-hatred. So, fill your cup, focus on your strengths, and find a safe haven within yourself.

Now that you've come home to yourself, and all the glowing qualities you embody, it's time to share your treasure with those around you. In the second part of this book, we'll discuss how to shed the mask of extroversion and begin revealing your inner irresistible to the world.

Part 2

Revealing Your Inner Irresistible

8

Peeling Back the Mask
of Extroversion

Many of us are familiar with the concept of a masquerade ball. We've watched countless movie scenes reenacting the lavish events. These decadent nights of mystery and celebration offer guests an enticing sense of freedom. High society and lower classes mingle without reproach. With the protection of masks and elaborate costumes, attendees can escape the constraints of a restrictive society for a night.

Introverts often wear the mask of extroversion so we can attend the extroverts' ball. Just like the high society of the Renaissance period, extroverts are seen as superior. Donning the cloak of extroversion, if only for a night, gives introverts a sense of belonging. We are free to mingle with the extroverts without being gawked at for our plainclothes personality. The subdued colors of our true temperament are too conspicuous for the extrovert's ball. So, we put on something more dazzling. We let our extroverted persona do all the shimmering and shining, while our true self hangs out in the shadows. This all seems safer than putting our authentic self out there.

When I was a child, I loved to play dress-up. From a young age, I lit up at the sight of all things sparkly. My obsession with sequins began when my mother put me in ballroom dance lessons when I was seven. I can vividly remember the first competition she took me to watch. I was instantly enchanted by the dazzling dresses. Bright sequined gowns with feather hems danced past, sweeping me up into another world, one that was infinitely more majestic than my own. The women who wore these elaborate dresses were like princesses from a faraway land. I wanted to try on their rhinestone shoes, slip into their satin and chiffon dresses, and slick back my hair into a shiny bun just like they did. I wanted to *be* them.

Later, I felt the same way about extroverted women. The world was friendlier to them, and vice versa. I decided the best thing to do was to play dress-up with my personality and put on a more sparkly persona.

Extrovert Envy

"They'll either want to kill you, kiss you, or be you."

—*Suzanne Collins*

My extrovert's mask was created out of envy. For introverts, it is all too easy to compare ourselves to extroverts and feel pretty lousy for it. Perhaps, we secretly wish that we could think on our feet like a fast-talking coworker. We might buy into the idea that chatty, bubbly women are more desirable. We become envious of the smooth-talking charmer that women flock to. As grown-ups, we know that jealousy and comparisons are destructive to self-esteem. But filling the gap between knowing and doing is no small task. It helps to remember that people who possess the qualities we lack aren't any better than us. They weren't given a bigger piece of the awesome pie. They are just as flawed, but in different ways.

I once had a roommate named Glory who was the epitome of extroverted charm. She was bubbly, popular, and always knew what to say. She was one of those people who are always on the go. Busyness is at the height of fashion in our culture, and she wore it well. What surprised me most about Glory was the roller coaster of emotions she stirred in me. Sometimes I felt envious of her extroverted charisma. Other times I felt inadequate. "Maybe I should be doing more," I thought to myself, feeling self-conscious about the gentler, slower approach I took to life. As time went on, a new sensation emerged when I was around Glory: aggravation.

I began to feel annoyed by her constant multitasking. I yearned for her to talk less, listen more, and stop changing the subject every other sentence. I realized that Glory wasn't the ideal woman I thought she was. She was just a different shade on the personality spectrum. She was fire-engine red, and I was pale pink. We all have our color preferences when it comes to painting our homes. Why would we want a world of only neon-colored personalities?

Coming Face to Face with Ourselves

Beneath every introvert's mask is our reluctance to accept ourselves. After all, the mask is the ultimate symbol of rejection of the self. If we can't even look ourselves in the face, who will? Much of the time, we feel bad about who we are because we are looking through the eyes of someone else. We let naysayers and critics sneak into our lives and distort how we see ourselves. Even well-meaning friends can skew our self-image with their own projections. Others describe us as shy, sensitive, and quiet. And perhaps we are, but we might also be social, silly, and bold, depending on the circumstances. Since other people are determined to flatten our complexity into two dimensions, we assume that is how it's supposed to be. We are one or the other: timid or vivacious, silly or serious, quiet or courageous. We forget that we can be all these things at once.

The question we must ask ourselves as we pull back our mask is: Who is the person beneath, and what is she hiding from? Masks and disguises, like any other armor, are constructed out of fear. The question is, fear of what? Fear of being seen, or fear of not being seen? Fear of rejection from those who don't even matter, or fear of acceptance by those who do? Perhaps, it is some confusing concoction of all sorts of irrational fears that seem to contradict one another. We are like toddlers fiercely fighting for our independence, while feeling terrified of abandonment. We cling to our facade because we don't want to be left behind.

Calling Back the Lost Parts

We're all too willing to exile our true personality if it means we can belong to someone, something, or somewhere. We've cast off the introverted parts and made refugees out of them. We sent our sensitivity to Africa to wander the Nile, while our intensity and intuitiveness trudge through a South American rain forest.

In Dr. Christiane Northrup's book, *Women's Bodies, Women's Wisdom*, she talks about how women who experience sexual trauma often disassociate from their body. A part of them is forced out, and sometimes it never returns. The same can be said for any kind of emotional trauma. It's as if pieces fracture off and flee. But we can call back the parts of our personality that have fled, even if we are the ones that sent them packing. The first step is to create space for them.

Like refugees who have been displaced for too long, our lost parts are eager to find a safe haven. We must clear out a space in our soul, empty out a sock drawer or two in our mind, and light a gentle fire in our heart, so these lost parts feel welcome and decide to stay. Right now it feels too crowded with all the extra layers of our personality. These tired little refugee parts of our true personality give us an ultimatum. "Us or the mask?" they question, as they back slowly toward the door.

For many of us, the answer seems clear on paper, but in real life it's not so simple. We have our jobs, our friends, and our reputations to think about. We see the mask as the glue that holds our life together. Without it, surely everything will crumble. Sometimes, we can strike a deal with our refugee parts. We can create some kind of cohabiting arrangement they can live with. The masquerade happens from nine to five, or five to nine, and they will have the place all to themselves for the rest of the time. I personally have tried this arrangement many times, and I didn't like it. It felt like I was stringing myself along. I was the two-faced playboy promising to make an honest woman out of myself, but never following through. Instead, I kept my true self waiting while I danced all hours at the extroverts' ball.

There is this New Age term called "holding space." It means to be there for someone in a fully present, nonjudgmental way. You create a little two-person sized bubble where they can feel safe, seen, and heard. The other day, one of my girlfriends came over for dinner and girl talk. She had recently been through a difficult breakup and needed someone to talk to. After sharing her story and shedding some tears, she looked at me with genuine appreciation and said, "You are really great at holding space.

Truly. Thank you." I've heard this before, as I'm sure you have too, if not in these exact words. Many introverts are wonderful at holding space for others, but don't know how to do it for ourselves. If we want our true selves to return to us, we must stop judging and start holding loving space for ourselves.

Our true self simply wants to feel seen and heard. It wants us to stop focusing on what's happening on the surface for a moment and face what lies beneath. The other day, I saw a group of otters playing on a floating dock near my house. They would climb onto the dock, scurry into a nearby speedboat, and then leap back into the water. Of course, I could only see them when they were at the water's surface. I found myself wondering what the otters were like underwater. Were they just as playful when no one was watching? What kinds of adventures did they go on in the depths of the ocean?

It's fun to ponder the mysteries of the natural world. For introverts, it can be just as satisfying to get curious about our inner landscapes. Curiosity is a powerful characteristic, one that many introverts naturally embody. When we get curious about what's happening beneath the surface of our own world, our true self feels liberated to come to the surface.

Leaving the Layers Behind

The problem with wearing a mask is that it is actually restrictive. If you've ever worn a full face mask for Halloween or, say, robbing a bank, you know how uncomfortable it can be. Shedding the mask feels a lot like being naked in front of someone you love. It's scary at first, but then it just feels so darn good to let the hidden bits of our personality hang out.

I experienced this feeling of letting it all hang out during my travels. When I first set out on my epic multi-continental adventure, I had two huge suitcases stuffed with clothes, shoes, and even dance costumes; "I might decide to join a dance team and perform with them," I reasoned. My love of all things sparkly was a liability while traveling. I cared too much about what I looked like to be traipsing around the world on a shoestring budget.

My first Couchsurfing host (I used couchsurfing.org, a website that helps travelers connect with hosts in their desired destination, and vice versa) found me quite amusing. He had hosted well over one hundred travelers from all over the world. "But you," he said with a chuckle, "are the first one to ever use my iron. I think you're the only one to wear high heels too." In my defense, I was going out salsa dancing that night, and dresses and heels make perfect sense in the salsa scene; in the nomad's world, however, not so much.

As the months passed, I gradually shed more and more items from my suitcase. Finally, a couple months into my journey, I decided to take a more drastic approach. When I reached Monteverde, Costa Rica, I set up shop by the side of a dusty road and sold an entire suitcase (luggage itself, and contents) for ten US dollars. I knew I couldn't carry on dragging so much baggage behind me. I looked and felt ridiculous. I tossed the heels and kept only plain, practical clothes. Makeup was minimal. Sequins, a distant memory. Once I had whittled down my wardrobe to what would fit into a slim carry-on and duffel bag, life felt lighter. For a girly girl with an addiction to dresses, I wore minimalism well. It was liberating to not have to worry about what to wear every day. I didn't have to "put on my face" every morning either. It all felt like a relief. There is a real lightness to living without so many layers.

As scary as it seems, peeling back the mask of extroversion feels good. Layer by layer, we unearth our true nature.

We reveal ourselves to the world and come face to face with whatever rejection follows. Rejection is part of the deal. The wrong people must fall away for the right ones to see us through the crowd.

Letting the Right People Find You

The mask makes it difficult for others to see beyond our facade. The right people can't find us, and the wrong people do. The danger of attending the extroverts' masquerade ball is that we surround ourselves with people who only like us for our disguise. After all, they can't feel affection for what they can't see. Oftentimes, we don't feel a true connection with the people we meet at the extroverts' ball either. We simply know that society has deemed extroverted behavior as the standard for which we should aim. We might find the typical extroverted form of communication overwhelming, and even irritating. But we view this as our shortcoming rather than theirs. After all, it's their party and we are merely masked guests.

We're afraid to even acknowledge our true preferences for fear that we'll be booted out of the ball. We want to have an in-depth conversation, but the party rules dictate that we must endure a substantial amount of small talk before diving into more personal topics. Sometimes, intimate conversations aren't allowed at all. Instead, guests gather in intimidating mobs and talk over one another. Their group banter sessions can carry on for hours. In such situations, we usually know what we don't want, but it can be tough to identify what we do want. If we don't want to be part of the extroverts' ball anymore, what is the alternative? What do we want instead?

Separating the Weeds from the Flowers

Often, introverts spend so much time trying to do as the extroverts do that we never ask ourselves what we really want. After years of denying our true desires, it can be difficult to separate what we want from what the world tells us to want. Doing so requires a shift in perspective. Imagine an open field of wildflowers, interspersed with dandelions. To a small child, the dandelions are no different than the flowers. They are equally vibrant and pleasing to the eye. To an adult, a dandelion is a weed. Its prolific growth is a nuisance. Same plant. Same field. Yet, the meaning assigned to the plant is completely different depending on whom you ask. The first step to reconnecting with our true desires is identifying the weeds and flowers in our own life. What is pleasing, and what is painful? Here are some questions to help you get started:

What would you be relieved to not have to do anymore?

Be specific. Instead of saying, "going to work every day," identify which aspects of your job feel painful. Is it your gregarious coworkers or the endless meetings where you have to hear these coworkers fight for airspace? Is it your jerk of a boss, or how your boss doesn't listen to you?

What about your spare time? Would you feel relieved to not have to see certain friends anymore or attend certain events? As much as the world tries to tell us otherwise, our free time is ours to spend how we wish. This can be a tricky concept for introverts to fully embrace. We've been chastised so much for our personal preferences that we feel obliged to ignore them.

What are you proud of right now?

As an introvert, you probably downplay your successes. You're not one to boast. But *if* you were to be proud of something right now, what would it be? I'm not just talking about your outward achievements, such as your certificates, degrees, and awards. Since introverts are intrinsically motivated, it makes sense to celebrate your inner accomplishments. How have you evolved mentally or emotionally over the past few months? What inner challenges have you overcome?

What could you get excited about right now?
Introverts tend to prefer a neutral emotional state to overwhelming highs and lows. For this reason, you might have trained yourself not to get excited. But feelings of excitement light the way toward fulfillment. You might also be tempted to believe that you should get excited about the same activities that extroverts get fired up over. It's okay to admit that you hate amusement parks. It's also okay to confess that you are really excited to spend Saturday night reading in bed.

What are you grateful for?
Gratitude practices are all the rage right now, for good reason. When we shift our focus to what we are grateful for, we inevitably seek out, attract, and enjoy more of these experiences. Most people like to make long lists of all the things for which they are grateful. Since introverts usually prefer to explore fewer topics in more depth, you might want to write at length about one or two things you are grateful for and why.

Sorry, I'm Not Sorry for Myself

One of the reasons that introverts continue wearing the mask of extroversion is that we feel like our true nature is something we need to apologize for. We are sorry for our need for space, our low energy, and our reluctance to jump on the party train.

In short, we are sorry for our introversion. Part of peeling back the mask is learning to stop apologizing for who we are.

You might have heard the stereotype that Canadians say "sorry" all the time. The truth is, we do. On several occasions, I've bumped into fellow Canucks and they were the ones who apologized. Likewise, I've caught myself saying "sorry" to people who have interrupted me or even walked in on me in the bathroom—"So sorry you caught me with my pants down!" We Canadians don't want to inconvenience anyone, and we certainly don't want to cause conflict. Introverts too are eager to apologize when, in fact, we are the ones being inconvenienced. The classic scenario to illustrate this would be an introvert who is trapped at a party just as her energy tanks are running dangerously low. Simply being around people at this point feels unbearable. She becomes irritable and edgy. The entire environment around her feels threatening. And yet, she is too busy feeling guilty to have a little compassion for herself. It's time for introverts to stop apologizing and start fulfilling our needs without guilt.

When we constantly apologize—even if only to ourselves—others start to believe we have a legitimate reason to be sorry. One of my mantras when I first started my blog was: "I never apologize for who I am." I don't apologize for my sensitivity, my quietness, my need for alone time, and I'm certainly not sorry that I tore up the extrovert's road map to follow my own path. The more the mantra became a part of my being, the less others questioned me. I encountered the dreaded "why are you so quiet?" question far less often. And when I did, I didn't let it bother me. "I'm enjoying listening," I'd say. Or, "I'm an introvert. I like people, but I get drained after a while."

Much like how dogs can sniff out fear, people can sense self-consciousness. They know if we feel guilty about a certain aspect of ourselves. They can read it in the curve of our spine, the shifting of our eyes, the slightest hesitation in our voice. Since people are more likely to believe what they see than what we say, we'd best get our story straight. Here is the CliffsNotes version: We are not sorry for ourselves. Period.

Showing the Underpants of Your Personality

It's difficult to stand there in our skivvies, the underpants of our personality on full display. It feels scary to be seen. For a woman, it's similar to the feeling of going out without makeup. During my churchgoing days, I heard a memorable sermon from a guest pastor from the South. Well, actually, only one part of his sermon was memorable: "A woman without makeup is like an unpainted barn," he joked, as those listening shifted in their seats, not knowing how to react. Regardless of how ridiculous his words were, they have stuck with me to this day. Now I wonder: if a woman without makeup is like an unpainted barn, what is an introvert without the mask of extroversion? Many of us secretly fear that we'll be like a dummy without its ventriloquist. Without our extroverted persona to animate us, we will cease to exist.

Though it is scary, it also feels wonderful to open up to the possibilities of our true personality after keeping it under wraps for so long. As I said before, the mask is limiting. Removing it creates new opportunities for growth, connection, and fulfillment. We can toss the mask and the itchy, chafing costume, and streak through the open fields of our true nature. As we distance ourselves from the extroverts' ball, we forget why we wanted to be part of it in the first place. Gradually, our self-consciousness is replaced with self-confidence.

9

Confidence Is an Inside Job

What do you think of when you hear the word "confidence"?

For me, the word conjures up images of women with wide smiles, big bright eyes, and a bubbly demeanor. I see smirking men strutting and backslapping with important people. I see groups of good-looking friends talking over each other, sharing one hilarious story after another and roaring with laughter. I see the popular girl at school, flipping her hair from side to side as she flirts with the guy with dreamy eyes. I see the cast of *Glee*.

Nowhere in this picture do I see myself, or any other introvert for that matter. The muted colors of introversion don't seem to match up with the stereotypical image of confidence. That's because confidence is often associated with extroversion. To be confident is to be bold, outgoing, and outwardly expressive. If we were to paint a picture of introverted confidence, it would look very different.

When I think of introverted confidence, I imagine a man with a stoic expression looking off into the distance with quiet determination. I see a smiling monk delighting in solitude. I see a woman dining alone, a look of unselfconscious satisfaction on her face. I see best friends sharing the same park bench as they journey to other worlds—one is traveling through the pages of a book while the other is transported by her paintbrush. I see Mona Lisa and her enigmatic smile.

I know several people who have gone to see the *Mona Lisa* at the Louvre. Most of them comment on how small the painting is in real life. They were expecting its size to match up to its level of fame. The *Mona Lisa*, painted by Leonardo da Vinci in in the early 1500s is, after all, the most famous painting in the world. Its countless reproductions are often much larger than the original. Those who have seen it in real life describe a painting not much bigger than an open newspaper, protected by bulletproof glass. Aside from its size, there are other aspects of the *Mona Lisa* that conflict with people's expectations. For one, the woman it depicts, believed to be named Lisa Gherardini, is not classically beautiful. Hers is a subtler kind of beauty. Her steady gaze and her "uncatchable smile," which shifts depending on which angle you view it from, draws us in. At first glance, she might seem like any other proper lady of her time. Nowadays, she would probably be described as uptight and too serious—a "prude." Her modest dress, reserved posture, and folded arms are in sharp contrast to the flailing exhibitionism that warrants attention these days. We must look closer to understand her appeal. One of the things I find most interesting about the *Mona Lisa* is that it did not truly become famous until the twentieth century. It slipped in quietly and grew on us over time.

I knew a girl in high school who was like this. Sarah said very little. She could often be found sitting along the edges of the room, nose in a book. At first glance, one might describe her as "homely" or "plain"—an Elizabeth Bennet type. But after a while, something changed. As a handsome acquaintance once commented, "When you first meet her, you don't really notice her. But then she kind of grows on you, and she starts to become really pretty." I knew exactly what he meant. I barely noticed her when I first met her, but after a while I began to see things I had overlooked before: the sincerity of her smile, the hint of green in her eyes, the freckles that only showed up in the sun. She really was pretty. We introverts have a way of growing on people too. We are the Mona Lisas and the Elizabeth Bennets. We exude a subtle kind of confidence that takes its time to pull you in.

There is another reason the *Mona Lisa* appeals to us despite its small size and seemingly plain subject. Leonardo purposely used contrast to draw us in. The darkness of her hair provided the perfect contrast for her pale skin. The shadowy background further illuminated her face. Introverts too are brimming with seemingly contrasting qualities. We are quiet and bold, sensitive and resilient, reserved and intense. We are both the moon that disappears into the dark and the sun that comes out to play. When I imagine a truly confident introvert, I envision someone in full ownership of these intriguing contradictions. Even the words "confident" and "introvert" might seem incompatible. In truth, they create a potent and powerful combination.

Now, we cannot leave a discussion about the *Mona Lisa* without saying a little bit about the frame. Its current frame was carefully selected to both flatter and preserve the painting. The *Mona Lisa's* flexible oak frame prevents warping, while its muted gold color complements the painting without over-whelming it. In the anatomy of a painting, the frame is the spine. It is there to support the mysterious movement of art to heart. The wrong frame will stifle the connection between painting and viewer. A frame that is too heavy, for example, might overpower a more delicate piece. The viewer doesn't notice the painting's quiet beauty because he is too distracted by the garish casing. Introverts are like this. We need the right frame to feel and appear confident. Unfortunately, many of us have been forcing ourselves into the wrong frame.

I feel embarrassed to admit it, but even after all these years creating articles, courses, and workshops designed to empower introverts, I still feel ashamed about my introversion in certain situations, namely, nearly any scenario where I am on extrovert turf and am outnumbered. It's one thing to feel proud of my introversion in the company of fellow introverts and quite another to do so while sitting at a noisy table or bar stool surrounded by extroverts. No matter how many times I visit extrovert turf, I still feel like an outsider there. At best, I remember that I am simply out of my element, and the extroverts would probably feel uncomfortable in my territory too. At worst, I slip into a state of self-loathing as I cruelly compare my worst qualities to their best ones.

In other situations, such as work-related activities and gatherings with close friends, I feel self-assured. These kinds of environments provide the perfect frame for my introverted nature. They allow my subtleties to shine through. For introverts, so much of developing confidence is about choosing environments that highlight our strengths. The outdoors is perfect for this. The tranquility of nature provides a flattering backdrop for sensitive souls who love to wander and ponder. While noisy pubs might make us look like "party poopers," quirky coffee shops and bookstores will show off our best qualities. Of course, it's not just about how others see us. When we place ourselves in the proper frame, we see ourselves for who we really are. We are no longer "the quiet one" or "the uptight one." We ease into our strangeness, seeing it as a strength rather than a stamp of inadequacy. An ex-boyfriend of mine used to tell me I was "quirky." He said it with such affection that I knew it was a compliment. When we allow ourselves to shine in the right environments, we begin to see our quirks with affection. We see that they are what prevent us from becoming flimsy reproductions of an extrovert original. We are above that. We are Mona Lisas.

Rooting for the Competition

We talked before about how introversion and shyness are not the same thing. Still, introverts are often shy in social situations. Shyness is related to fear. Many introverts develop a fear of socializing because of repeated failures in the past. We went to a social activity and we were told that we were doing something wrong. Perhaps we were too reserved and not talking enough. Even if we weren't told implicitly that we were getting it wrong, we could see it in other people's facial expressions and body language. We noticed the way they shifted impatiently as we spoke, looking for an exit from the conversation. We could see how their eyes skipped over us, as if we were invisible. Eventually, we wished we were.

Sometimes, our fears seep into aspects of our life where we should feel successful. After all, confidence is the assurance in our abilities. It's the belief that we are enough. If we are told that we are inadequate in one area of our life, before long we believe we're deficient in every area. Even if we are good at something, we place our bets on the other (often more extroverted) guy.

I have a pesky habit of rooting for the competition. In grade five, I was astonished when I was chosen for the lead role in our class play about a monkey named Marvin. I thought surely Melanie Stevenson should have been chosen to play Marvin. When I was given the part, I felt guilty, as if there had been a mistake. I felt the same way when I found out I had made the

Century Club (an annual award for the top one hundred students in my high school) for the first time. Another boy, who I thought was smarter than me, complained that the courses I took were easier than his, which was the reason why he hadn't made the club. I felt so bad that I went to the principal to ask to be excluded from the honor. He did not oblige, and I went on to be part of the club each subsequent year until I graduated. It was the same thing with men. I always assumed the man I liked would be better off with someone else. I would meet these other girls and think, *She's so much more interesting and fun than me. He should be with her.* I took myself out of the race before the gun sounded, then cheered for the girl with the most enthusiastic stride.

Part of developing confidence is going in with a winner's mind-set. Instead of rooting for the competition, we acknowledge what we have to offer. This is not always easy for introverts, who tend to go into interactions with what I call a "beggar's mind-set." That is to say we think that people are doing us a favor by talking to us. In the back of our mind, we're telling ourselves, "They don't really want to talk to me. They're just being polite." When we think this way, we come off as either aloof or insecure. Instead, confidence emerges when we go in with a giver's mind-set. Rather than thinking we are taking something away when we talk to a person, we imagine we are giving them something of value. Believe it or not, our time and attention are precious. When we go into conversations knowing we are offering people a gift by being truly present with them, we naturally exude a self-assured vibe.

Creating a giver's mind-set begins with focusing on our strengths. As we discussed in Chapter Four, we can choose which thoughts we give our attention to. Rather than focusing on the little troll in our head who tells us we have nothing to offer, we do some digging and pinpoint exactly what it is we *do* have to give. These don't have to be tangible gifts, like money. They don't even need to involve action. Sometimes introverts don't realize what a gift it is to simply share a space with someone else and let them see us just as we are. We're always so quick to rail at ourselves for our quietness, as if we're poisoning the air with silence. But a calm and quiet demeanor is refreshing. It is such a rare thing in this world to find someone who is not constantly trying to impress someone, be liked, or fill empty airspace with mindless chatter. A person who is completely, unapologetically okay with who they are and what they feel is like a beacon of light in the dark. As author Anne Lamott once said, "Lighthouses don't go running all over an island looking for boats to save; they just stand there shining." Here are some other gifts of introversion to keep in mind when you feel like you have nothing to offer:

- Creativity: Embracing solitude and reflection helps introverts access our innermost thoughts and creative ideas.
- Observation: As outsiders, introverts often notice subtleties that those who follow the crowd miss.
- Loyalty: Introverts are known for being fiercely loyal to the few people we let into our inner circle.
- Deep thinking: Introverts tend to carefully think things through before acting, which often prevents negative outcomes.
- Listening: Introverts embody the old adage, "You have two ears and one mouth for a reason." Everyone likes to be listened to.
- Focus: We are able to maintain intense focus for long stretches when we work alone on a project or passion.

- Introspection: Our love of looking inward helps us to continuously learn and grow.
- Word economy: While others may talk mindlessly about everything and nothing, introverts choose our words wisely.
- Love of being alone: Introverts don't need to be around people all the time. Our love of being alone gives us both independence and perspective. When we honor our need for alone time, we can share the boons of our self-exploration when we reconnect with our loved ones.

Sort of Confident, Sometimes

The interesting thing about confidence is that it isn't always evenly distributed throughout our life. We might only have a tiny dollop of confidence in social situations, while a big scoop is heaped onto our work life. Similarly, we could be completely at home on stage performing in front of hundreds of people, then feel painfully awkward at the post-show party. This was the case for one enormously talented jazz legend. At the height of her career, this famous songstress confidently shared the stage with the likes of Louis Armstrong, Charlie Parker, and Dizzy Gillespie. There was a time, however, when no one, not even the singer herself, could have believed that she would one day command the stage with such poise. Ironically, stage fright was the impetus for her future success.

At sixteen, the shy songstress entered a competition at the Harlem Opera House. She had intended to dance, but felt inadequate after seeing that the two dancers who went before her were more talented. She froze with fear the moment she stepped on stage. Knowing she had to do *something*, she sang a Hoagy Carmichael song called "Judy," and then followed it with "The Object of My Affection" by Connee Boswell. She won the competition and decided to become a singer.

That shy and frightened teen grew up to be the great jazz legend Ella Fitzgerald. The surprising part of the story is that she never completely shook her self-doubt. She has been described as having very little self-confidence, though you'd never know it if you saw her perform. As pianist Billy Taylor put it, "She never really believed that she was Ella Fitzgerald." Doesn't that statement ring true for so many of us introverts? We don't believe that we are as talented, smart, gifted, worthy, or loveable as people say we are. Only when we are in our chosen roles, whether that be on stage, at work, or at home, do we reluctantly accept that we are good enough. Even then, we might be placing our bets on the other guy.

This kind of confidence—the kind where we are self-assured in one area of our life and insecure in others—is called "situational confidence." Most people have some degree of situational confidence; however, for introverts, it can be especially confusing. We can't figure out why we are sometimes awkward and inhibited, and at other times self-assured. Those around us are quick to label us as shy, but we know there is more to it than that. See if this story sounds familiar:

When I was in college, I worked at a deli in a specialty grocery store. Caroline, the manager of the deli, was the best boss I've ever had. She was a natural leader, confident and authoritative, yet empathetic. I assumed that her self-assured manner extended to all areas of her life. Then one day, a work event gave me the chance to see a different side of Caroline.

Every summer, the store held a staff picnic at a park. When I saw Caroline there, I was astounded by what I beheld. This wasn't the self-assured, assertive woman I knew at work. This

Caroline was retracted and shy. She resembled a new driver who hadn't read the instruction manual for her own body. She stood away from the group, folding her arms between drags of her ever-present cigarette.

When we spoke, I noticed that her facial expressions and voice tone were different too. Her words were stilted; her face pinched and pulled down into a frown. Caroline had an obvious case of situational confidence. She was confident at work, but insecure in other social settings. Josh, a former student of mine, had a similar kind of situational confidence. He explains:

> I feel most comfortable at work because I feel like I'm in control of these areas. It's something I've been practicing or doing for almost ten years now at the same company. I know who to go to for information, or to get something done. I feel comfortable at work because I also feel well respected. My work ethic has helped me create a name for myself, and, because of that, there's a sense of pride that if I don't know something, I can figure it out.

I'm sure a lot of introverts will relate to Caroline's and Josh's situational confidence. It is natural to feel more at ease in certain circumstances. But when we develop what is known as "core confidence," our self-esteem is spread out more evenly.

Developing Core Confidence

Core confidence emanates from the inside out and is not dependent on circumstances. This means that no matter where we are or whom we are with, we feel good about ourselves. We trade constant self-deprecation for a steady stream of internal high fives. Going back to our previous lighthouse analogy, lighthouses continue shining regardless of the circumstances. Even in the middle of a sunny summer day, they keep on shining. Core confidence is like this. It endures through any situation. So, how do we go from shaky situational confidence to core confidence? The first step is to explore why we lack confidence in certain circumstances.

The reasons surrounding our situational confidence might be obvious or they might be more elusive. We know we are self-assured at work because we have achieved a lot in this area. We know we are less confident at parties because we are intimidated and overwhelmed by big groups. But what about when it comes to relationship dynamics? Why is it that we feel insecure when our partner has more friends than us? What is it about spending time with our parents that stirs up feelings of adequacy? One way to better understand our uneven confidence is to identify the things that throw us off center.

Imagine a master tightrope artist who rarely loses his balance. The wind can blow and the audience can cheer, but his feet will stay solidly planted on that rope. Even if some chump gives him a little shove and he wavers, he'll quickly regain his footing. Core confidence is much the same. When we have it, few things throw us off balance. We are firmly grounded in our own self-worth. We know our values and boundaries. We know where others end and we begin. People who possess this kind of confidence are actually quite rare. Most of us have a number of invisible triggers that throw us off balance without us even realizing it. A trigger is something that causes a reaction in us that is disproportionate to what has occurred. It is that hidden little button that, when pushed, unleashes a flurry of strong emotions. Naturally, these emotions are tied to areas where we feel shame and guilt—otherwise, why keep them locked up? Let's look at an example:

Graham was a client of mine who had recently started dating again. During one of our sessions, the usually calm Graham became agitated and angry as he described a date he had been on. He talked about how the woman had given him mixed messages. In his eyes, she had been deceptive about who she was and what she wanted from him. Fair enough, but why was it that this woman, who he admitted he didn't even like, had the power to cause such a major reaction in Graham?

After exploring the matter further, we uncovered that the reason this woman so infuriated Graham was because he felt she had betrayed his trust. He then admitted that issues with trust were a common theme throughout his life. A close family member had deceived him early on. Over the years, the pattern of betrayal repeated itself again and again. His trust issues influenced every area of his life, the way he dealt with his colleagues, his friends, and even me. The moment a woman showed any sign (real or imagined) of being untrustworthy, he was infuriated. His reaction seemed out of sync with what was actually occurring. In other words, he was triggered.

As a colleague of mine once jokingly remarked, "If you're not sure what triggers you, spend a weekend with your parents and it will quickly become apparent!" Another way to tell what triggers you is to think back to the last time you felt strong, negative emotions like anger, shame, or self-loathing. Ask yourself:

- What was it that stirred such a strong emotional reaction in me?
- What other circumstances have stirred similar feelings? What was the cause then?

It is important to be mindful of our triggers because these are like flashing red lights pointing toward our deepest shadows and insecurities. Once we know what is throwing us off center, we can start strengthening our core against it.

Overcoming Your Fears

Famous actor and comedian Will Ferrell used to be painfully shy. He chose to take an extreme approach to overcoming his fears. "In college, I would push an overhead projector across campus with my pants just low enough to show my butt. Then my friend would incite the crowd to be like, 'Look at that idiot!' That's how I got over being shy." Ferrell faced one of his biggest fears head-on. While this method can work, it can also backfire, making us even more anxious than we were before. Unfortunately, many people believe Ferrell's head-on approach will work for everyone. These are the people who tell us to "just put yourself out there" and "get out of your comfort zone." It sounds simple enough. However, just like diving straight into freezing cold water, jumping into a social situation that scares us can be a shock to our system. Introverts are better off starting with small, achievable goals that stretch our comfort zone instead of obliterating it.

Rather than force yourself to spend two hours socializing, begin with ten minutes. Instead of approaching new people right away, start with an inviting smile. Leave it at that until you feel ready to try a new challenge. If you're not ready to put yourself out there at all, then start with a visualization. Imagine yourself walking into a room with confidence and saying "hello" to a friendly-looking person.

Fear is not entirely a bad thing. Courage cannot exist without fear. Often, it is the fact that we are frightened out of our wits that motivates us to follow through. Like many introverts, I over-prepare in the face of fear. This characteristic has helped me to develop many talents that would have otherwise lain dormant. Sometimes, however, our fear gets in the way of what we want to do. Instead of motivating us, it debilitates us. Things that seem simple to others, like talking to someone new, setting boundaries, or sharing our truth, can be a real struggle. We have experienced failures in these areas in the past. How can we be sure we won't fall flat on our face again? The solution is to give ourselves proof.

Find examples of success in your past and focus on those. Recall a time when you introduced yourself to someone new, and they received you with warmth and appreciation. Perhaps, you are still friends with that person to this day. Make a note of every tiny step you take to move past your fear. See it like a game of golf. You are walking the course at your own pace, and every swing counts. No one expects you to get a hole in one every time.

As you leave behind the extrovert's portrait of confidence, remember that introverted confidence is not a contradiction. It begins with a clear decision to stop rooting for the competition and start recognizing your many gifts. Once you know your strengths, you can begin highlighting them by choosing the right frame. One small step at a time, you face your fears, knowing that many great introverts have gone before you. Some of them looked like smiling monks. Others resembled the poised, yet mysterious Mona Lisa. Confidence can also look a whole lot like the person you see staring back at you each time you look in the mirror.

10

The Inner Game of Intrigue

"She wasn't doing a thing I could see, except
standing there leaning on the balcony railing,
holding the universe together."

—*J. D. Salinger*

During my salsa dancing days, I spent a lot of time watching dance performances on YouTube. In one particular video, a young woman competes in a salsa solo competition. She sweeps across the stage, spinning and stepping in time with the fast-paced music. Her movements are bold and bright. If she were a comic book hero, her performance would be punctuated with plenty of POW-WHAM-WOWs. At one point, she does a cartwheel into a split—POW! Then she spins in place and strikes a pose—WHAM! She manages to do all of this without falling out of her teeny tiny gold, sequined costume, which looks more like a sparkly bikini than a dress—WOW! It's not just her movements and outfit that scream for attention. Her facial expressions are just as over the top. Her mouth stretches into a smile, opens wide as if to bite a giant burger, then narrows into a come-hither pucker.

Most people would never believe that the woman in the video is an introvert. But I am certain that she is. I should know, because the woman in the video is me. Really, she is my own version of Beyoncé's Sasha Fierce. She is the character I've created to embody all of the wild vivaciousness I normally keep hidden. There is no denying that this version of me receives a lot of attention. A better way to put it would be to say that she *demands* a lot of attention—*look at me! Look at me! I'm dancing!*

In real life, I would feel uncomfortable seeking attention in this way. A two-minute performance is one thing. Doing a daily song and dance for attention is quite another. Like me, most introverts would feel strange being so bold in their everyday interactions. Yet, this is how we are told charisma should manifest. It should instantly demand that you look at it, listen to it, and desire it. In many social situations, introverts are more likely to wish not to be seen than to behave in a "look at me" sort of way. Though we might not want to be the center of attention, a little notice from the right people would be nice. We know that trying to be bold and gregarious doesn't work so well for us. But neither does pretending to be invisible. There is another approach, which strikes a balance between the two extremes. Best of all, it comes naturally to introverts.

Intrigue

Intrigue is the ability to arouse interest. It is the means by which we peak a person's curiosity and draw him or her in. It is subtler than flattery and charm, which rub against our legs like a cat purring for attention. The ability to intrigue emerges from the inside and needs little outer action.

A lot of introverts waste time trying on every style of extroverted charisma, cramming ourselves into personas that are entirely the wrong shape and size for us. We don't realize that we already have everything we need to be compelling. When introverts tap into our inner intrigue, others are drawn to us like children beckoned by the sweet scent of apple pie wafting from our kitchen windows. As if hypnotized, they follow their nose straight to the source of the spiced perfume. They might not know what's cooking, or if it will taste as delicious as it smells, but they intend to find out.

In the same way, intrigue entices without telling everything. We keep our poker hands close to heart, while offering just enough information so those around us want to keep playing. There are a few subtle but effective ways we do this. In this chapter, we'll discuss four essentials for being irresistibly intriguing. As you read, you might feel a hint of nostalgia as you recall a time when you did these things naturally. That's because these are concepts that play to an introvert's innate strengths. You'll likely slip right into them as you would a dress or tailor-made suit that is just your size.

Expression

We touched on emotional expression in Chapter Six; however, this topic deserves deeper exploration as it's a key element of intrigue.

I've heard people say that introverts are natural actors. Since we've played the role of extrovert for so long, we are very good at pretending. The only problem with this reasoning is that a good actor does not pretend. I once heard Academy Award–winning actress Jennifer Lawrence say in an interview that she always knew she was different growing up because she had an intense form of empathy. She felt the emotions of others deeply. If they cried, she cried. Just thinking about an experience could bring on a wave of emotions. Nowadays, she channels her ability to feel on cue into her work. She doesn't *pretend* to feel sad, happy, terrified, or angry. She lets the emotions rise up within her. She feels the sadness until real tears come. Likewise, she feels the anger until her eyes blaze and her muscles tense.

An amateur actor isn't so good at this. She forces out emotionless tears as if drawing from an empty well. Her focus is on her face, her gait, and the placement of her hands. These all matter, but without the internal change, she is like a hollow hand puppet. It is the same with all forms of expression. Our feelings, characters, minds, and souls seep out through our voices and facial expressions. They become our poetry, our music, and our movement. This has nothing to do with pretending.

Why is it, then, that so many of us think pretending to be extroverted is the key to expression? We believe that to win the golden statue, we must express ourselves in bold and dramatic ways. When it comes to authentic expression, bigger is not necessarily better. I've heard that TV actors (especially those in sitcoms) usually speak loudly, projecting as if onstage. Movie actors speak more softly. In movies, the focus is on the subtleties of emotion rather than grand gestures followed by studio applause. This kind of expression doesn't bark at you for attention or reach out and grab you by the collar. It quietly compels you to draw closer until you are totally absorbed. To be so enchanting, we must first be enchanted. This is usually no problem for introverts.

Introverts like to climb into the center of things and find their meaning. When we satisfy this urge, others become curious about us. They want to follow the flames of our passions right down to the wick to discover its origin. The catch is not to become so absorbed that we are oblivious to the world around us. When we completely disconnect, we are no longer expressing so much as we are obsessing. One of my favorite classes in college was modern art history. I was captivated by the cubist creations of Picasso and the surrealist world of Dalí. More than anything, it was the concepts behind each art piece that fascinated me. Expressionism, a modern art movement inspired by works such as Edvard Munch's *The Scream*, challenged artists to create from within. Rather than making art that mimicked the external world, the focus was on the internal feelings of the painter. Their works brought their invisible inner world to the surface, where others could engage with it. Most introverts have a vibrant internal world, rich with broad strokes of emotion and imagination. But we don't know how to bring any of it to the surface. Our greatest masterpieces stay hidden.

Actually creating art—prose, photographs, quilts, sketches, etc.—is one way to express our internal thoughts and feelings. If we are willing to be vulnerable, we can also let art light us up. For example, when we visit our favorite gallery, we let the paintings speak to us or touch us so deeply that our emotions come to the surface. This doesn't mean we cheer for joy or wail in agony right there in the middle of the gallery, while a tired-looking security guard signals for us to quiet down. We simply stay present with whatever we are feeling and let the emotions emerge in their own quiet way. This kind of communication with art makes what is normally unseen seen. It gives those around us an idea of who we are and what matters to us. Truly engaging with nature, music, or a physical activity will have a similar effect. Our passions will start to show on the surface, and others will take notice.

A common misconception about expression is that it needs some kind of applause. Because we live in a highly outcomes-focused society, we believe our worth is dependent on what we can produce or achieve. The one with the most accolades is thought to be the most successful. But authentic expression is not about getting a high five or a gold star. Artists feel most fulfilled when they appreciate the process regardless of the outcome. The writer goes on writing despite a few bad reviews. The painter continues to paint even if some pieces never sell. Contrary to what our culture tells us, outcomes are not everything. Expressing ourselves through our passions will not always impress people. Some won't even bat an eyelash as we divulge our souls. And they certainly won't always give us a pat on the back. We express ourselves simply because it feels good to *us*. On top of that, authentic expression will provide opportunities for connections with the right people.

When it comes to expression, a small amount can go a long way. Luckily for introverts, this is one of those instances where less is more. We don't have to be over the top for others to take notice. In fact, our calm demeanor makes any form of expression that much more intriguing. I know a lot of people who go around expressing every passing thought and emotion. After a while, nothing stands out. All the words and revelations melt together like a really long run-on sentence.

Many people believe that the more you do and produce, the greater impact you'll have. This is not true. Most of the time, only a small portion of what we put out there really matters. The 80/20 rule explains this concept well. The premise of this rule is that 20 percent of the work we do creates 80 percent of the results. So, if we focus on that 20 percent, we can do a lot less work and get the same, or better, results. With regards to expression, we don't have to spend eight hours a day putting it all out there. A small amount of focused, authentic expression will have a greater impact instead of running around all day oozing emotions out of every orifice. There will also be fewer cleanups afterward.

The Push–Pull of Magnetism

When we think of a magnet, we usually picture its attractive quality. We imagine its ability to pull objects toward it with a powerful, invisible force. But there is another equally powerful property to consider: the push. If you try to put two magnets together, they will repel each other. It is this push–pull quality that makes magnets fascinating. This same concept of push and pull can be used to stir up intrigue.

Introverts naturally need and want to pull away sometimes. We go quiet to gather our thoughts or disappear for a while to daydream. The tricky part is finding the balance between "the push" (distancing ourselves from people) and "the pull" (drawing them closer). First let's explore the pull and what that looks like for an introvert. Imagine this scenario:

You are at a party and an interesting stranger approaches you. You practice being fully present, listening carefully to what they say. You are in what I like to think of as a "receiving mode." The other person has stepped into your introvert bubble, and you have welcomed them. They are sharing things with you, and you are adding your own insights. Being in the receiving mode feels natural for introverts. It is just as natural for those around us to be drawn in like magnets. Now, let's see what the push might look like:

You are growing tired of conversing. You politely excuse yourself and begin exploring your surroundings. You step out onto the balcony and take in a sky of stars, completely content in this stolen moment of solitude. Next, you slip back inside and find a safe space to observe the scene. You perch yourself on top of an overstuffed ottoman and watch the room. Your time on the sidelines allows you to refuel. Something else happens during your voluntary time-out. People become curious about you. They wonder, *Who is this person who confidently stands away from the crowd? What are they thinking? When will they return to us?* This is the power of the push.

It's very easy for introverts to get stuck in either state. Often, we find ourselves wedged in the middle of a draining conversation. We might desperately want to dislodge ourselves from the interaction, but instead we stay in receiving mode, absorbing their words like a slow-acting poison. On the other hand, we might pull away too quickly and spend the entire evening hovering self-consciously along the sidelines. We become cranky and prickly, pushing everyone away in one fell swoop. When we push too hard, the pull becomes null. Usually, this happens when we show up with empty energy tanks. We guard the last of our energy reserves with the fierceness of a mama bear protecting her cubs. This is incredibly intimidating to those who don't know us well.

We've already covered how to manage energy levels quite extensively in a previous chapter, so we won't get into it too much here. The most important thing is to prioritize energy restoration so we don't experience mama bear aggression in the middle of a party. If we do find ourselves running on empty, it's best to either go home or do a quick recharge by going for a walk. Distance from people is crucial at this point.

Mastering the push–pull of introvert magnetism is all about owning whatever state we're in. When we are in the receiving mode, we fully embrace it: we let people in, we listen, and we offer our own insights. When we are in the push, it's important to resist the temptation to feel guilty or self-conscious. Instead, we relish our time to observe and restore. Even though we have removed ourselves from the thick of things, we stay curious and present, proudly inhabiting the edges like night watchmen with an important job to do.

Owning the Room

One of my brother's good friends is married to a flight attendant. Shauna has been a flight attendant for well over a decade now. The last time I saw Shauna and her husband was at my brother's wedding reception. When I walked into the Chinese restaurant where the reception was held, I saw Shauna standing in the foyer. With her shining blond hair and brightly colored dress, you couldn't miss her, especially amidst all my conservatively dressed Chinese relatives. Like a greeter at a church, she smiled at everyone who entered. One of my cousins said that when she first saw Shauna, she had assumed she was a hostess who worked for the restaurant. I have never seen a non-Asian hostess at the traditional Chinese restaurants where we have our family gatherings. I was surprised that anyone could have mistaken Shauna as an employee. I suspect her profession had something to do with it.

As a flight attendant, Shauna was used to warmly welcoming people onto the plane, as if she were ushering them through her own front door. Wherever she was, she had a similar vibe. Her posture and energy said, *This is my space, and I want you to feel welcome here.* In other words, she felt a sense of ownership of her surroundings. Introverts can take on a similar mind-set when it comes to socializing. This is not about *appearing* to own the room, nor does it have anything to do with slapping on a smile and shaking hands with anyone who walks through the door. What we're talking about here is a shift in the way we see ourselves relative to our surroundings.

Imagine for a moment that you are someplace where you are completely in your element. Perhaps it is at the climbing gym. Or maybe it is your work environment. It could also be your home. You feel naturally comfortable in these settings. People who visit these spaces for the very first time will not feel so at home. If you are an empathetic person, which many introverts are, you will want to put these newcomers at ease; after all, you have the upper hand. The interesting thing is that the new person immediately senses that you have been here before. Just as the senior students in a high school have a more seasoned vibe, you give off an air of been-here-done-that to all newcomers.

As introverts, we can become instantly more compelling by choosing to see ourselves as the seasoned veterans in a given situation. To do this, we don't actually have to be more experienced or in our element. A shift in mind-set is all that is needed. When I first started attending a large Pentecostal church as a teen, I felt totally out of my element. On a given Sunday, several hundred people would shuffle in and out of the rows and rows of wooden pews. The youth group alone had over sixty regular attendees. I should note here that the teenage years are not typically a good time for introverts. On top of all the usual teen worries like pimples, popularity, and whether or not our crush knows we exist, we also fret about our introversion. At least, that's how it was for me.

As a quiet and introspective teen, I felt decidedly uncool amidst all the loudmouthed extroverts who dominated the youth group. Even after months of attending, I still felt like an outsider. Then, something occurred to me. If I felt like such an outcast, maybe others felt this way too. I remembered my fellow fringe dwellers in the youth group (loners, geeks, and kids who came from broken families). Many of them had complained about feeling unwelcome. I made it my mission to change that. I decided that anytime I saw a new face at church, I would go up to them and say hello and do my best to make them feel welcome.

Like many introverts, I usually prefer to wait for others to come to me. Initiating conversations with complete strangers was out of character. However, something about attaching a worthwhile purpose to my actions made me follow through. I was surprised at how confident I felt as I took on the role of welcome wagon. Around the popular kids in the youth group, I disappeared into the background, too shy to put two sentences together. Yet there I was, smiling at strangers and inviting them to come sit with me. Countless people would later tell me, with genuine gratitude, that I was the first person to make them feel welcome and accepted at church.

The reason this was possible was because I saw myself as the person on higher ground. From this position I could easily lift others up and, in doing so, elevate my own confidence. A lot of introverts put this concept into practice without even knowing it. We do this by becoming facilitators, group leaders, or organizers. These kinds of roles give introverts who are normally socially passive the push to be more proactive in our interactions. We feel a sense of ownership of our meetup group, book club, or outdoor adventure group. Our desire to make others feel accepted starts to overpower our fear of being rejected.

We don't need to be in a designated role to take ownership of our environment. We can simply decide that we will be the giver, the helper, or the greeter wherever we are. We can even make a little game of it. We can tell ourselves: *Today, I'm going to make at least three new people feel welcome.* Or we can say: *At this party, I'm going to gift two people a genuine compliment.* In this way, we trick ourselves into doing something that we secretly wanted to do anyway, since most of us really do have good hearts. Beneath our outer shell is a compassionate side, soft as the belly of a kitten. We want those around us to feel good. Or perhaps, we simply just don't want them to feel bad. We want to spare them the agony of walking up to a group of strangers and being completely ignored, or going to an event and feeling like no one is interested in meeting them. The solution is simple: take the higher ground, and while we're up there, extend a hand to the newbies, freaks, geeks, outcasts, and loners who make their way to our patch of grass.

Presence

We've touched on how presence can help introverts stop overthinking. Being fully awake to the present moment also makes us more attractive and engaging. Without presence, we look at people without ever really seeing them, and we don't give them the chance to truly see us, either. To be present is to feel our breath, our body, and whatever sensation another person stirs in us. We could be doing absolutely nothing—barely moving an eyelash or uttering a single word—and be irresistibly compelling simply because we are fully present. I'm reminded of a documentary I saw called *The Artist Is Present*. It follows the famous Serbian performance artist Marina Abramović as she prepares for a major retrospective of her work at the Museum of Modern Art (MOMA) in New York.

"Marina seduces everyone she meets," says Klaus Biesenbach, Abramović's ex-lover and MOMA chief curator. Though stunning for a woman in her sixties, it's not Abramović's physical appearance that makes her so enticing. In her three-month-long performance piece at MOMA, we see the essence of her seduction.

Abramović sits at a table for several hours at a time as individuals from the audience line up to take the coveted seat across from her. There is no talking or overt communication of any kind, just Abramović's pure presence. Abramović and the audience member enter into what the raven-haired artist calls "an energy dialogue." Audience members are clearly moved by the exchange. Some laugh with delight, others cry. Most are seduced by her ability to reveal herself in the rawest of ways. Emotions, energy, presence—all undressed and placed on the table for the world to see. This level of presence is rare.

A lot of introverts tend to leave the present moment to go mind wandering. Meanwhile, those around us notice the vacant look on our face and realize that we're not really with them. To be more present, start experiencing the moment through your senses. Relish the feel, smell, and taste of what is happening right now. When your mind starts to wander, bring it back to the subtle or strong sensations of the moment. If you are someone who tends to be in your head a lot, feeling your experiences through your senses won't come naturally. You have to consciously practice the art of presence. Start today by noticing how things feel on and within your body. Notice the texture of your clothing and how it feels against your skin. Bring your awareness to the pressure of the hot water on your body when you shower. When you are with others and you start to daydream, return to the present moment by focusing on your tactile sensations or the gentle rise and fall of your chest as you breathe.

There is another aspect of intrigue that you might not have considered. As we draw a person in, we give them the chance to see the world from our unique perspective. This has always been my favorite part about traveling. Seeing things from a different perspective makes life feel fresh again. It's like pushing the reset button on our well-worn beliefs. Through presence, we too will get a snapshot of the world from a new point of view. Authentic expression is the invisible chemical reaction that develops our Polaroid picture. Meanwhile, the push–pull keeps others interested as the image develops. In this way, intrigue invites learning, expansion, and deep connection— all this without ever having to force ourselves into oversized personas. Or tight, sequined bikinis.

11

Your Voice—the Gateway to Connection

When I was younger, I used to get a lot of colds. The first sign of infection was a tight feeling in my throat, which later turned into a tickle, and then a cough. Sometimes, the cold never fully set in. It curled up in the warmth of my windpipe for a day or two, and then left. Though I didn't get sick, my throat was sensitive for days. It also began to sound hoarse, as if I had swallowed sand. The few words I spoke came out too textured, scuffed by the grainy remnants of my cold.

Looking back, I see a lot of parallels between my frequent sore throats and the way I used my voice. When I spoke, I often felt like the words got stuck in my throat. Either that, or they squeaked out in uneven tones, like the jagged edge of a saw. When I caught a cold, it was as if all my unsaid sentences had accumulated in my throat, forming a big yellow lump of phlegm. I don't know about the sickness part, but I'm sure a lot of introverts can relate to this feeling of having blocked vocal passageways.

If our eyes are the window to the soul, our voice is the doorway. For introverts, it often feels more like a narrow gate through which words may or may not sneak out. We don't think of our voice as a reliable form of expression—that is, if we think about it at all. Much of the time, we view our voice as a necessary tool that we can never quite master. Truthfully, we haven't really tried. We push a few buttons, turn some knobs, and hope for the best. This is unfortunate because our voice says a lot about who we are. More accurately, our voice is an inherent part of who we are. I'm reminded of a piece of writing advice I've come across again and again over the years: to be a good writer, you must first find your voice. This implies that the voice is an integral part of our being. It channels our values, our experiences, and our sense of humor. Our voice says much more about us than, say, our legs, or even our smile. When we open up our vocal cords, we also open up opportunities to be seen and heard. Isn't that what we all secretly want? Yet, in daily life, the voice is taken for granted, misused, and manipulated.

When I was an adolescent, one of my girlfriends and I would huddle by the phone late at night and leave messages on one of those 1-800 chat lines. It was free for women who were eighteen and older, so we deepened our voices and tried to speak in a sexy, raspy tone. We didn't actually intend on meeting any of the lonely male voices on the other end (thank goodness!). It was all a big joke to us. We knew these mystery men would never meet us in person or even see a picture of us. To them, we were just muffled voices in the dark, and vice versa.

Back then we used our voices like playthings that didn't matter. Some of us never outgrow this attitude. We manipulate our voice to please whoever's listening on the other end. Drastically altering our voice doesn't seem as extreme as changing our physical appearance. After all, it's just air passing through a folded membrane or two; what's the big deal? But the voice is so much more than this.

The Power of the Voice

Our voice has the power to delight, thrill, and transport. In shamanic and Buddhist traditions, certain intonations of the voice are used to channel energy through the mind-body-spirit circuit. In parent–child relationships, the voice marks the passage of time, each age giving way to a change in vocal tone. We feel the power of the voice when we hear the lilting laughter of a loved one. We give into the power of the voice when we are seduced by the dark, husky tones of a lover.

In Greek mythology, the story of the Sirens illustrates how the voice can be used as an irresistible form of seduction. The Sirens were beautiful creatures that lured sailors off course with the sound of their enchanting voices, causing them to shipwreck on the rocky coast. Most of us wouldn't want to use our voices for such extreme purposes. We don't mind the seduction part, but we would rather not kill our conquests in the process. Really, we just want to use our voice to connect with others. A better way of putting it might be to say we want our voice to use us. Our voice is like an independent entity, formed in our belly and delivered on the wings of words. It's something inside us that wants to come out—an emotion, a dream, a desire for belonging.

To better understand the power of the voice, let's revisit the woman behind one of the most famous voices in history: Ella Fitzgerald. Fitzgerald had perfect pitch, and could "play" her voice like a musical instrument. She had a nice, round sound, plump and perky in the way it hopped along each note. It could also be smooth and rich, like a dark velvet robe against bare skin. I wanted to know how Ella Fitzgerald might have felt while singing on stage, so I asked my friend Narissa, who is a jazz singer, what it feels like when she performs. "Connection," she replied, "both to myself and to the audience." Each note she sings onstage is saturated with an emotion or intention. These little vocal intentions dance through the air like a charmed cobra, inviting each audience member to sway along. This is the essence of the voice's power—it is an invitation for connection.

I first started to recognize the important role our voice plays in making connections when I started hosting teleseminars. These are voice-based online seminars, which I share with my website audience. I immediately noticed a shift in the way my online community responded to me after I started hosting teleseminars. I received a fair amount of comments on my voice. Some were as simple as, "I like your voice." Other comments were more specific, touching on what aspect of my speaking resonated with them. Many said they appreciated that I spoke slowly and clearly, making it easy to follow along. One student who spoke English as a second language said, "I found your expressions . . . easy to understand; you talk slow[ly] and clear[ly]."

I'm sure some people who listened to my teleseminars didn't really like my voice. But those who did reached a new level of connection with me. They had already connected with my writing voice, and now they knew what I sounded like. They could hear all sorts of things within my vocal tone and inflections: excitement, nervousness, warmth, confidence, and whether or not I was genuine. For a lot of people, hearing my voice built a sense of trust between us. I know this because my first handful of students signed on right after listening to me speak on a teleseminar, even though I had been promoting the program (an audio course) for a week through my blog and email marketing.

A lot of us can appreciate the power of the voice when we hear others speaking or singing. But when we hear our own voice, we are not so impressed. *Do I really sound like that?* we wonder.

Perhaps, we sound more high-pitched than we imagine, or more nasal. We don't want to listen. We want to switch off the recording and go back to pretending that our voices don't matter. I've already established that it really does matter, though not in the way we might think.

Speaking with Vocal Resonance

It is generally accepted that the voice signals how confident and assertive we are. According to popular opinion, a loud, deep voice indicates power and importance. On the other hand, a soft, high-pitched voice says, "I'm not very important, confident, or smart, so don't pay much attention to me." These stereotypes lead introverts to believe that simply deepening our tone and turning up the volume will make us more appealing; however, the qualities that make a voice attractive are more complex than this. Loudness often has nothing to do with it.

Morgan Freeman has a uniquely attractive voice. The Academy Award–winning actor is now just as famous for his narration work as he is for his acting. It is not the loudness of his voice that gets our attention. Much of the time, he speaks softly. People are drawn in by the texture of his voice, which is as rich as molasses. He speaks slowly, stretching out each vowel into long raspy strands, then pausing to emphasize his point. Freeman is smooth—so smooth that he doesn't need to speak in a booming voice to make us listen.

The important thing for introverts is to find the tone and volume level that suits us. In other words, we must find our resonant voice. Again, this doesn't necessarily involve speaking more loudly. When people say, "that resonates with me," what they really mean is that they can relate to it. Our words, our truth, and our voice reverberate within their body, like an echo. Finding our resonant voice is a lot like this. We speak in a tone that makes our words vibrate most strongly within us. The vibration we feel is the sensation of the voice echoing in one of our body's resonant cavities.

The earlier analogy of Ella Fitzgerald playing her voice like an instrument is actually quite literal. The body is similar to several acoustic instruments in that it has hollow, air-filled chambers that resonate as we speak or sing. The main resonating chambers are located in the chest, throat, the front of the face (often called the "mask"), and the head. Each chamber produces different tones, which can be associated with corresponding colors. Chest tones sound rounded and dark, while mask tones are bright and high-pitched. The voice is usually the most vibrant and pleasant to listen to when we resonate in the mask. Even if we speak quietly, our voices will sound clearer with mask resonance.

Finding our resonant voice isn't just about pleasing others. Using the right vocal tone will put less strain on our vocal cords. Both loud and quiet speaking can cause vocal strain when we are not using our resonant voice. In his book *The Awakened Introvert*, my friend and colleague, Dr. Arnie Kozak, shares the story of how he developed a functional voice disorder from using his voice in an inefficient way. To cope, he would speak more softly, but this only caused more strain. "I had to learn to talk again to change the energy in my voice, and to move my voice from the lower throat to the space around my nose and mouth," he said. In other words, Dr. Kozak had to learn to speak with mask resonance.

Buzzing Bee Exercise for Vocal Resonance

An introvert friend and colleague of mine, introvert speaking skills specialist Jade Joddle, has a great exercise for finding your resonant voice.

1. Pinch the fingers of your right hand together and move them in front of your face, neck, and chest as if your pinched fingers are a bee that is flying around in the air. Now, make a buzzing sound like a bee. Imagine that you are locating this sound where your fingers are pinched together.

2. As you move your pinched fingers around, as if they are a bee, change the frequency and resonance of the buzzing (this might feel tricky at first; experimenting is key).

3. Change the pitch of the bee from high to low. It helps to lift your eyes up when doing a high pitch and to look down to do a low pitch. As you do this, pay attention to how the vibrations in your body also change.

4. To get more experimental, imagine how it would sound if you were to swallow the bee. Imagine that the bee flies inside your mouth, down into your chest, and then back out of your mouth again. In what way does the imagined sound of the bee change as it explores the inside of your body?

5. Fly the bee near your nose and mouth. Make the vibrations you feel here as strong and loud as possible.

Project the buzzing sound forward from your mouth by about two inches. This location is where you can project your normal speaking voice in order to make it sound richly resonant.

6. The sounds that have the most resonance are "m," "n," "b," and "v." Exaggerate the resonant sounds in the following sentences:

I am a busy bee.

My voice is yummy honey.

Be happy, bee.

Doing the buzzing bee exercise may cause tingles to happen in the mouth area; this is a good thing, even if it does feel odd at first. Such tingles are a sign that we have increased the range of our everyday voices. With practice and awareness, this change flows into our daily speech to make it more rich and sonorous.

The Breath

Those of us who have given a speech or presentation know how important it is to breathe when we speak. It's amazing how such a simple autonomic function becomes difficult when we're nervous. We take short, shallow breaths, and then barely finish half a sentence before running out of air. We sound like an engine that's sputtering to an unexpected halt. It's not just public speaking that stints our breathing. Many of us always breathe inefficiently. We don't take in enough air to support our speech.

Most of my life, I have been a shallow breather. This started to change a few years ago when I experienced a kind of spiritual awakening. I had been listening to audios of various spiritual teachers and doing nightly meditations and visualizations. After about a month of this, I suddenly felt an overflowing sense of peace and vitality. It was like I had been half asleep and the universe came along and performed mouth-to-mouth on me, breathing life back into me. After my revival, I stopped sipping air politely. I took giant, greedy gulps and enjoyed every breath. My voice changed, too. Before, I often pinched off my airways in an effort to make my voice smaller and less obtrusive. Now, whenever I speak I let the air pass smoothly through my vocal cords.

My new way of breathing and speaking is all about fullness: deep full breaths, smooth and round sounds, lungs and heart overflowing with life. I was speaking slightly louder, but the real difference was in the tone and texture of my voice. I spoke in a clearer, deeper tone. Before, I had been too afraid to access the fullness of my resonant voice. As if frightened by my own truth, I used to hide in the higher tones. Though the effects of my spiritual awakening have worn off somewhat, I'm still mindful of my breathing. I've noticed that when I am practicing yoga and meditation regularly, deep breathing comes more naturally.

Another way to improve our breathing is to focus on phrasing. When I was a little girl, I took vocal lessons for a couple of years. My teacher always made me pencil in the stops and commas in each sentence of a song. This reminded me when to breathe. Since one breath had to carry me smoothly through an entire phrase, I had to make it count. "Breathe from your diaphragm," my teacher would say, as she gently pressed her hand over my belly. (The diaphragm is a dome-shaped sheet of muscle located in the lower ribs. It is the powerhouse of respiration.)

It turns out that the very same vocal training that applies to singing also applies to speaking. When we speak, all of our words should be connected in one fluid phrase. Proper breathing is essential, lest we collapse before finishing our sentence. How and when we take those breaths is also important. It helps to focus on filling our diaphragm with each breath, then allowing that breath to connect every word until we reach a comma or stop. It might take practice to do this without sounding like we're gasping for air. Here is an exercise to get started:

Diaphragmatic Breathing Exercise

Part One

Start off by lying on your back. Place one hand on your chest and one hand on your diaphragm (about two inches above your belly button). Take three deep breaths in and out as you normally would.

With the next three to four breaths, focus on filling your diaphragm. The hand that is on your stomach should rise and fall with each breath, while the hand on your chest should stay still. If your chest is rising with each breath, it means you're using the muscles in your neck and chest to support your breathing.

Part Two

Sit up straight with your feet planted firmly and evenly on the ground. Relax your shoulders, and place one hand on your chest and one on your diaphragm (just as you did in part one). Once again, take three to four breaths in and out, while focusing on filling your diaphragm. This might feel more difficult now that you are sitting up. It should feel like you're inflating an invisible balloon inside your stomach. The air goes in smoothly and swiftly just like it does when you see a balloon being filled by a helium machine.

Tone

Now, let's talk more about tone. Our vocal tone, which consists of the pitch, character, and quality of our voice, transmits a lot to those listening. It conveys our mood, our emotions, and our message. This is especially obvious when we talk on the phone. I'm sure you've experienced this scenario:

You pick up the phone (you know, that dreaded apparatus you normally try to avoid at all costs) and call a new friend. You've spoken to this friend a few times in person, but never over the phone. You are caught off guard when she answers. "Hello," she says curtly, followed by a clipped, "What's up?" Her tone is low and colorless. Maybe you've interrupted her? Or perhaps she simply despises the phone as much as you do. You begin to feel self-conscious, like you've done something naughty, but can't pinpoint what. "Is that all?" she asks, as the conversation begins to wind down. She is letting more and more air into her words now, blowing them out in dusty clouds. Her words say one thing, but her tone says another. It is telling you that she is annoyed, tired, hates your guts, or all of the above. Then you realize something unsettling: She sounds exactly how you probably sound every time you receive an unexpected phone call.

I give this example not to induce feelings of guilt but to illustrate the kind of messages our tones can convey. The phone emphasizes vocal tone because we have no visual cues to draw on. A few people have told me that I sound grumpy and intimidating on the phone. This works to my advantage when solicitors call. With friends, however, I'd like to sound more inviting. Luckily, it's not very difficult to brighten our tone. Aside from speaking in our resonant voice, we can also enhance our tone by focusing on inflection.

Inflection is the act of modulating tone. Instead of speaking in a dull monotone, we change our pitch. If our voice were an instrument, we wouldn't want to hammer away at the same note all the time. That would be boring. Likewise, we don't want to speak on the same "note" for an entire sentence. Celebrity vocal coach Roger Love, of www.theperfectvoice. com, likens vocal tones to keys on a piano. He says that far too many people are monotone (one note), while some only use about two to three notes when speaking. To sound more interesting, competent, and confident, Love recommends using eight to twelve keys in a progressive fashion without predictable rhythms. Changing our voice intonation maintains interest because people naturally tune out predictable sounds when they assume they already know what's coming next.

An easy way to assess your vocal tone is to record yourself speaking. As you listen, pay attention to the messages your tone is sending. How many keys are you playing on your voice piano? What emotions are conveyed? Next, record yourself again, but this time try using a variety of notes. It might help to imagine that you are your favorite talk show host or sports anchor. Don't be afraid to sound foolish. Exaggerate, and be over the top. Now, as you're listening to the recording, assess how you sound compared to the previous recording. Do you sound happier? More confident? More intelligent? You might be surprised at how much you can exaggerate your tone without sounding weird or inauthentic.

The Wrong Environment for Your Voice

Sometimes, no matter how well we play our vocal piano, we just can't seem to escape vocal strain. We work in busy extroverted work environments all day and come home with sore vocal cords. This was the case for Maria, a student of one of my introvert courses on energy. She explains: "I have been signed out of work with laryngitis. More proof, if I ever needed it, that I am in the wrong job as an introvert. My job involves talking all day and my voice has just given up now. This quiet time out will give me a chance to recoup and conserve my energy. Very ironic, considering I'm doing your course at this time."

I can definitely relate to Maria's struggles. Before I started my blog Introvert Spring, I worked in several customer service jobs (bank teller, waitress, medical assistant, and coffee shop manager, to name a few). I realize now that the vocal strain I felt during and after work was caused by energy drain. Working in extrovert-oriented environments all day is exhausting. When our energy is low, our breathing is shallower. This causes us to use our voice inefficiently. If we are working in a career where we must talk a lot, we don't get the chance to relax our throat and reenergize. By the end of the day, our voice is cloudy and hoarse, a sure sign that we have been straining our vocal cords.

I've also noticed that my vocal tone changes depending on whom I'm speaking with. If I'm talking to someone who is loud and tends to interrupt, my voice shrinks and gets higher. On the other hand, when I'm speaking with someone who listens well and speaks at a volume similar to mine, my vocal cords relax and I settle into my resonant voice. Many introverts are similar to me in that their voices change depending on the circumstances. If this is the case for you, make note of the times when you speak with your most natural, unstrained voice. You'll know because you will sound clearer and your throat will feel relaxed. You will likely find that your resonant voice emerges most with your dearest friends, as well as in environments where you feel the most competent.

In Stephen King's book *On Writing: A Memoir of the Craft*, he talks about resonance. "What I want most of all is resonance, something that will linger for a little while in Constant Reader's mind (and heart) after he or she has closed the book and put it up on the book shelf." While King wants to achieve resonance through his stories, we want to do so with our speech. We want our voice, along with the messages it carries, to linger within another person. Otherwise, why bother? To achieve resonance, both within ourselves and those listening, we must get quiet enough to hear our own inner voice. This is where introverts are at an advantage. Just as we have come to enjoy the sound of rain falling outside our window or the gentle creaking of wood floors, so, too, can we appreciate the sound of our own voice in the dark, or even (gasp!) over the phone. So, take a deep breath, open your vocal gateway, and let your most resonant voice be heard.

12

The Language of the Body

As introverts, we have a tendency to be so much inside our head that we don't notice anything else, including our own body. We are like bodiless brains that float around on a hovercraft of thoughts. This might sound like fun, but there are side effects to the constant disconnect between body and mind. The most obvious one is that we literally feel disconnected. We lose touch with what our body is trying to tell us. This means that others can't figure out what our body is trying to tell them either.

The language of our body is created by the connection between our body and mind. When we are present within our body, we listen to it, feel its sensations, and notice the signals we would sometimes rather ignore. Playwright, author, and activist Eve Ensler wrote about her disassociation from her body and how cancer forced her to inhabit her own flesh. She writes: "Because I did not, could not, inhabit my body or the Earth, I could not feel or know their pain. I could not intuit their willingness or refusals, and I most certainly never knew the boundaries of enough." Most of us can relate on some level to what Ensler is saying. When we detach from our bodies, we detach from our intuition. Our "gut feelings" aren't so strong when we ignore our gut. We can't "follow our heart" when our entire torso is merely a prop for our brain.

When we are truly inhabiting our body—paying attention to it, moving it, using it in ways that feel good, and listening to its whisperings before they turn into a shout—we are inside our primary vehicle for connection. And we are at the steering wheel. I often have dreams that I am driving, and I lose control of the car. The wheel seems to spin itself, and the brakes don't work. This is the sensation of disassociation from our body. Our limbs don't do or say what they're supposed to. Our rigid arms send a message that our curled spine contradicts. Our feet do a tap dance while our head does a nosedive. Our eyes shift in every direction as the rest of our body pulls on the emergency brake.

Sure, we can control the messages our body conveys by doing power poses and developing better posture. These are both good things that will help us get back in touch with our body. But going straight to posing would be leaping ahead several steps. Let's not worry about what our body is telling others right now. First, let's focus on what it's telling *us*.

During my teens and early twenties, I felt disconnected from my body. Many factors contributed to my disassociation from my body, but two stand out most: my discomfort with my introversion and my rigid religious views. My guilt and shame over my quietness, sensitivity, and low energy made me want to hide inside my head. My body was merely a shell to protect my battered ego from further rejection.

My religion (Pentecostal Christian, then Mormon) made me view my body as a temple that was to be kept pure. I honored and respected it in the same way I would the Queen of England—from a distance, and with more a sense of duty than genuine affection. The focus was on keeping my body covered and chaste. Sensuality was saved for the marriage bed.

The thing is, it's hard to separate the way you view your body with your spouse from the way you view it the rest of the time. Mostly, I saw my body as something mechanical—a tool to be used as needed and maintained according to instructions (eat, sleep, poop, exercise, wash, rinse, repeat). I would take my body in for its yearly tune-up, then put it on cruise control and crawl back inside my brain.

I started to view my body differently after I got divorced and got off the religious path. Around this time, I started salsa dancing. This is what really helped me to reconnect with my body. I was suddenly more aware of the sensual aspect of my body. Sensuality has to do with the gratification of the senses; it's not necessarily sexual. Still, many definitions of sensuality tie it to a lack of chastity and morals. The general message I received during my religious years was that sensuality was naughty (except under very specific circumstances, and in moderation, of course). No wonder I felt so distant from my body.

The Messages within Movement

If our body is a vehicle, our sensations are the steering wheel. They guide us toward vitality, pleasure, and connection. When I started dancing, my senses told me it was time to enjoy the pleasure of movement. You might have felt a similar sensation after a divorce or some other major life change. Subconsciously, we want to match external shifts with internal shifts. We want to start moving things within us. We want to circulate stagnant fluids, sweat out old emotions, and dance into a new mental state. This all sounds lovely and poetic, but it does require some discomfort. Namely, we must get off our asses and actually start moving.

I know, I know. You were expecting me to give you some quick body language tips that you could try out for a day or two, then promptly forget. You might still be a little hazy on what movement has to do with charisma. If so, I must ask:

Have you ever been in complete awe of a bird flying, a dancer stretching her limbs, or a fighter throwing punches so fast they're a blur? It's not just the movement that fascinates you. It's the sweat and determination, the creation of art right before your eyes, the endorphins that you can almost see exploding from their bodies, the sound of air moving in and out and in and out. All of these things tell you that this person is very much alive. When you feel that quiet voice prompting you to join them, it is not so much that you want to become a bird, a dancer, or a fighter. You just want to share in their aliveness.

We are attracted to lively people because we, too, want to feel alive. There is a misconception that lively means extroverted. This is not true. Movement is just one shining example of this. We don't have to be outgoing to move. We can move in the privacy of our home or our nest in nature.

The evidence of our movement will remain even as we are still. Just as regular yoga practice changes the posture, gait, and breathing of a yogi, so, too, will any form of movement change the way we feel and appear in all circumstances—yes, all. This includes a party, a team meeting at work (you know, those weekly time wasters you dread), or a family gathering. As the saying goes, "Wherever you go, there you are." This, by the way, is the title of Jon Kabat-Zinn's popular book on mindfulness meditation. I remember coming across the title a couple of years ago and thinking, *Duh*. But now I understand. We bring our perspective, our thoughts, our emotions, and—the glorious casing for all these things—our body into every circumstance. If we can't be at peace with all of the above when we are alone, we won't truly be at peace with it when we are with others. Movement ensures that, wherever we are, we look and feel like someone who loves to walk in nature, stretch into backbends, or do high-intensity interval workouts. Such a person usually looks and feels more confident and content than, say, someone who sits at a desk all day and on the couch all night. I have been both the former and the latter. Speaking from experience, being the person who moves is an instant confidence boost.

Each of the forms of movement I've mentioned will have a different feel and effect. Some might make us feel like we are in a head-on collision with our own body, muscles and joints jamming together like crushed metal. Others will be as easy and relaxing as wading into warm water. Different movements will also send distinct messages to others. Think of the bodybuilder and the tight, controlled way in which he moves at the gym and elsewhere. Think of the ballet dancer and her straight back and graceful stride. Even in his seventies, my tai chi–loving Chinese grandfather moved with a lightness of foot that said more about him than a thousand words would. If a picture is worth a thousand words, a moving picture must be worth, I don't know, a zillion? (Math has never been my strong point, by the way.)

The other thing about movement is that we don't have to pigeonhole ourselves. There is no strictly introverted or strictly extroverted way to move our bodies. We might be tempted to assume that introverts would want to keep our movements small in public, so we don't draw attention to ourselves. At times, this can be the case. But many introverts secretly yearn for the right opportunity to move in broad strokes. In Susan Cain's book *Quiet: The Power of Introverts in a World that Can't Stop Talking*, she talks about her experience at a Tony Robbins seminar. Robbins's "Unleash the Power Within" seminars are notoriously high energy. He gets you up and moving, jumping and dancing in the aisles as if you were at a Pentecostal revival meeting. One would expect Cain to say that she was horrified. We imagine that she spent the entire time planted in place, doing her best to be invisible. Initially, Cain does resist the hype, standing peevishly with her arms crossed as other participants clap and dance around her, but soon she joins in. And then, the most shocking part of all, she actually enjoys herself. "I've always loved to dance, and I have to admit that gyrating en masse to Top 40 classics is an excellent way to pass the time," Cain writes.

There are plenty of introverted athletes, dancers, and actors who relish using their bodies in bold expressive ways, especially if there is an audience. In other situations, these same people might feel inhibited and self-conscious. This makes them all the more appreciative when they find the right stage for their movement. After all, movement is one of the most powerful ways to circulate, express, and release strong emotions. There is a video of a *haka* at a wedding reception that has been making the rounds on social media. The *haka* is an ancestral tradition of the Māori people of New Zealand. It involves vigorous movements and shouting, as well as exaggerated facial expressions. Māori warriors originally performed *haka* before a battle to show their strength to the enemy. Nowadays, *haka* are also performed during various celebrations and rites of passage.

In the video, about twenty or thirty men, all in shirts and ties, are gathered in the center of the reception hall, half on one side and half on the other in a sort of face off. They grunt, yell, and pound their chest. They also stick out their tongues, but not in a nana-nana-boo-boo kind of way; they thrust their tongues straight down toward the bottom of their chins, stretching their entire faces and making their eyes bulge. I wouldn't say their movements are angry, though they do seem aggressive. In *haka*, different parts of body are used as instruments to express emotion. The face is a key part of the harmony. Facial expressions are exaggerated, not just to intimidate opponents but also to make the warriors feel powerful. The whole thing is pure emotion from beginning to end. Their movements and facial expressions are so raw and intense that I can't look away.

What really gets me is when the camera focuses on the bride. She is obviously feeling it, breathing in the potent musk of emotion. At one point, she begins to cry. This is different than your typical happy bride cry. This is the cry of a woman who feels overwhelmed by the joy of knowing she is part of something bigger than herself. I think this is the essence of the *haka* tradition, or any tradition of movement and expression for that matter. It's not about war and division. It's about strengthening the connection between our fellow soldiers and us. Toward the end of the *haka*, the bride and groom join in. This is my favorite part. The *haka* is often thought of as a male tradition, but women partake as well. The bride, delicate in her white dress and rose head wreath, does not hold back. Pulsing her arms, she lifts the world in a bicep curl, and then punches the air with her battle cry. It is mesmerizing.

We introverts can also store a surprising amount of emotion in a seemingly delicate frame. Movement helps to circulate these emotions while naturally connecting us to others. Thankfully, we don't have to put ourselves on public display to reap the benefits of movement. In fact, we don't even have to be particularly mobile. A large aspect of movement is internal. Air, fluids, feelings, and thoughts are always making their way through one part of our body or another. Even small outer shifts will influence our inner flow. My New Year's resolution in 2016 was to focus on movement. My main objective was to liberate old emotions and beliefs, then evict them from my body and mind. On New Year's Day, I got out a big square of white paperboard and a black Sharpie. I jotted down the words "Body," "Voice," and "Mind." For each category, I brainstormed possible activities. Here is what I came up with:

- Body: Zouk (a form of dance), cleanse, sweat, sauna, massage, AcroYoga, squash, bike, walk, meditate, run, kayak
- Voice: Singing, speaking engagements, webinars, videos, podcasts
- Mind: EFT tapping, BodyTalk therapy, complete *The Irresistible Introvert* (I did it!), new models, new beliefs, new story

I focused on both external and internal movement. Many of the activities I came up with involved very little physical exertion. The actions under "Voice," for example, were concerned with the movement of air and emotions. The "Mind" activities were focused on circulating stagnant thoughts and releasing outdated beliefs. Even some of my ideas for the "Body" category involved little outer movement. Both sweating and meditation can be done sitting still. In the end, everything I brainstormed is connected—the internal, the external, the air, and the emotions all run together like watercolors.

If you have been sedentary for a while, you might feel resistant to the idea of adding more movement to your life. One thing to remember is that movement doesn't have to mean exercise. This is key because a lot of us have all sorts of apprehensions when it comes to exercise. We hear phrases like, "no pain, no gain," and think, *Okay, no gain it is then.* We prefer mental self-flagellation to physical, thank you very much. Thankfully, movement doesn't have to be painful. It can be relaxing, fun, expressive, artistic, and so much more. Most importantly, movement helps create connection with both ourselves and those around us.

Posing and Postures

There is a lot of advice out there about power posing. You might have seen Amy Cuddy's famous TED Talk on how our body language affects our brain. Cuddy is a social psychologist whose research shows that we can change the way we feel and appear simply by changing body positions. She talks about how "power posing," adopting the stances associated with power and confidence, can affect testosterone and cortisol levels in the brain. In other words, power posing can literally make us feel more powerful. The interesting (and comforting) thing about her findings is that these poses can be done alone. This is good news for introverts who might feel unnatural striking a pose in public. According to Cuddy's research, power posing for as little as two minutes at a time can change our brain chemistry. Doing so was shown to reduce cortisol, the hormone associated with stress, and increase testosterone, the hormone linked to feelings of confidence.

Facial Expressions

Our face is one of the first things people notice about us. Introverts tend to forget this simple fact. We let our face do its own thing, allowing it to settle into what I like to call our "resting bitch face," the facial expression we default to when we are concentrating, daydreaming, or focusing intensely on something.

We glare, wrinkle our brows, and let our lips fall into a frown. To the outside world, it might appear that we're upset, but we're not necessarily angry or sad. We might be having a wonderful time frolicking through enchanted imaginary worlds in our minds. Or perhaps we're simply observing a person or event with catlike focus. Regardless of what we're thinking about when we default to our resting bitch face, others are sure to misinterpret our facial expression. Some people will self-consciously assume that we're judging them. Others will think that we are depressed. Many people, as I'm sure you've experienced, will take it upon themselves to "turn our frown upside down."

Smiling is a powerful connection tool, if our emotions match our face. Otherwise, we risk coming off like robotic news anchors who smile on cue. I once knew a man who was like this. No matter what he was saying, his mouth stretched into a wide grin. After a while, his perma-smile started to get on my nerves. There was no glow behind it. The lights were out, and I could find no flicker of true feeling with which to connect. I couldn't tell if he was happy, sad, angry, or constipated. It all looked the same. At best, I was disinterested by his fake facial expression. At worst, I felt total distrust. Don't get me wrong, I have nothing against the occasional forced smile to put a stranger at ease or stop a baby from crying. But if it's true connection we're after, any contrived facial expression will work against us. It becomes just another way of trying to solve an inner problem with an outer quick fix. Even if we're great actors, our micro expressions will give us away.

Micro expressions are brief, involuntary facial expressions that display a concealed or suppressed emotion. "Micro expressions happen when people have hidden their feelings from themselves (repression) or when they deliberately try to conceal their feelings from others," says Dr. Paul Ekman, renowned psychologist and a co-discoverer of micro expressions with Friesen, Haggard, and Isaacs. "Importantly, both instances look the same; you cannot tell from the expression itself whether it is the product of suppression (deliberate concealment) or repression (unconscious concealment)."

Even though micro expressions only last one-fifteenth to one-twenty-fifth of a second, they can be spotted. Ekman actually offers a course on his website on how to detect them. Often, observant introverts naturally notice fleeting facial expressions. This, of course, means that others can pick up on our micro expressions too; so much for trying to "fake it till you make it." Ekman's research shows that a fake smile won't fool the people who are paying attention. I don't know about you, but I want the kind of friends who can look me in the eye and see through my bullshit.

If we can't hide our feelings with our facial expressions, what is the alternative? It's quite simple, actually: 1) Change the way we feel 2) Be okay with displaying true feelings on our faces. The third option, and this is my preference, is to do both. If something doesn't feel good, we explore why. Often, we can easily shift our emotions by changing our thoughts. Other times, we need to tweak our outer circumstances. This could mean ducking away to find a less stimulating atmosphere or simply turning down the stereo volume. Then there are moments when there is no way around it; we just have to feel what we are feeling and let our face do its thing.

Naturally, we don't want to intimidate or turn off others with our facial expressions. Rather than slapping on a happy face that doesn't match my feelings, I prefer to focus on openness. I open up my face by looking up and letting my eyebrows, lips, and jaw relax into whatever shape they want to take. This feels different than hiding behind a forced smile. It looks different too. An open facial expression says, "Come on in, the house is a little messy right now, but I won't judge if you don't." A fake face is a closed door.

Now, what about our eyes? Most have heard about the importance of eye contact. Looking people in the eye establishes trust and connection. Many introverts have no problem looking people in the eye while they are listening; however, we often have trouble keeping eye contact when we are talking. The reason is that introverts are not verbal processors. We need to think before we speak.

What do most people do when they're thinking? They break eye contact and look up or off into the distance. This is natural, but it does make it harder for people to connect with what we're saying. Experts say that maintaining eye contact between 60 to 70 percent of the time is ideal for creating rapport. We don't have to hold someone's gaze the whole time we're talking (that's creepy). Looking away here and there for a couple of seconds is natural.

Now that we have the most important stuff out of the way, we can talk about the more traditional body language pointers. These are straightforward, though they can take practice. Here are some tips to keep in mind:

- Lowering your head (as if bowing) when talking is a sign of submission. This means that you will seem less self-assured than someone with a straight neck. Exude more confidence by keeping your chin level with the ground and your shoulders square.
- Tilting your head to the side is also a subtle sign of submission. Since it can also indicate curiosity and interest,

doing it every so often isn't necessarily a bad thing. Just aim to have a straight neck the majority of the time.

- Confident people take up more space than those with low self-esteem. They expand their chest and let their elbows jut out. To start, try unfolding your arms and resting them casually by your side. When you're standing, spread your legs a little bit further apart instead of crossing them or holding them tightly together. If you're a woman, you might prefer standing with your legs staggered and your weight on your back leg, as this is a confident and feminine position.
- Introverts tend to wander around with our heads in the clouds. Sometimes, we're so immersed in thought that we don't know where we're going. Add confidence to your step by walking with intention. Instead of shuffling around and looking at your feet, choose your end destination and aim straight for it.
- It's important to be on the same level with those you are talking to. If they are sitting, sit or kneel down. If they are standing, rise to their level. This way you can speak eye-to-eye. Mirroring your conversation partner's body angle is also essential. If they are facing you head-on, align your chest with theirs. If their chest is angled slightly away from you, angle yours out as well.

Again, the above tips work best when we first reconnect with our body and listen to the messages it has for us. Then, through conscious movement, we can change the way we feel in our own body as well as how we appear to others. In this way we inhabit the driver's seat of life's most important vehicle. And we'll already be well on our way toward the true connection we desire.

13

Crossing the Circle—Lessons in Introvert Dating

Remember how I mentioned earlier that I used to feel like an outsider in my kindergarten circle? It wasn't just because I was an introvert. Puppy love also played a part in my feelings of alienation. In senior kindergarten, I had a crush on a boy named Kyle. He made my little four-year-old heart do twirls, so one day I decided to do something about it. I mustered all the courage my three-foot frame could carry, walked across the circle, and plunked myself down next to Kyle. As soon as I sat down, Kyle got up and walked to the opposite side of the circle to sit beside his friend. And thus began my lifelong habit of admiring my love interests from afar. I've noticed that a lot of introverts share this habit. We set our sights on someone special and then we do what we do best—we keenly observe our love interest from a distance, unbeknownst to him or her.

While others blow kisses to their crushes, introverts try desperately not to blow our cover. We really know how to put the "secret" in "secret admirer." Though our affections stay hidden on the outside, they proliferate like fruit flies on the inside. Thanks to our overly active imaginations, our fantasies become more and more elaborate. Though we might have plenty of imaginary conversations with our crush, in real life we barely speak to him or her. All the communication conundrums we face as introverts—thinking of the punch line five minutes too late, speaking slowly, and getting tongue-tied—are amplified in the company of someone we like. The words are unreachable. It's as if all our fantasies have woven together to form a net over our thoughts. The net tightens in our crush's presence. We want to speak to him or her in the here and now, but the fantasies get in the way. What can we possibly say to this demigod of our own creation? Apparently, not much.

Extrovert Mating Calls

We would like to have some of that extroverted charm that seems to turn its nose up at our tongue-tied ways. We envy the way some extroverts can walk right up to the person they like, open their mouths, and let whole, fully formed, coherent sentences tumble out. There doesn't appear to have been any prior planning. The words are formed right there and then and sent down the conveyor belt to their desired destination. The quality control may be lacking, but the point is that they get their thoughts assembled and out into the world where attractive guys and girls can receive them with smiles, laughter, and scintillating eye contact. Sometimes it involves touching too, but not the creepy, groping kind. Instead, there is a gentle press on the elbow, a squeeze of the forearm, a brush of the hand, a lean in with a giggle, all done with casual finesse as if they have been snuggling up to intimidatingly attractive people since birth (perhaps their mothers were the original Real Housewives).

In our youth, we behold the extrovert flirting process in the same way we would some strange animal mating ritual:

The male extrovert calls to attract a female. He juts out his elbows and flexes his arms to impress her. Then he lets out a confident mating call, which consists more or less of descriptions of what he did on the weekend, plus a few generic compliments: "There's just something about you." The female extrovert leans back to consider his display, while at the same time baring her teeth and giggling to convey interest. Viewing this as a signal of attraction, the male extrovert makes his move, pulling out his large smartphone to complete the ritual. The rite complete, both female and male extroverts retreat to their respective clans to recount the exchange.

Observing extroverts in action can make us feel envious. How can that which appears so natural for them be so hard for us? Of course, flirting is easy in our fantasies. The words flow effortlessly and our movements are smooth and casual. In real life, our body has a way of detaching from our brain when talking to the object of our affection. Movements become stilted. Words get lodged in our throat. Seeing others flirt with ease makes us feel like we are on the outside of the circle again, excluded from the flirting club. Jealousy is born out of feelings of exclusion and deprivation. We want what we think we cannot have.

We've seen enough. We're determined to figure this whole flirting thing out. We would also like to go on dates without having to worry about our brain floating away from our body, taking any coherent thoughts along with it. Is that too much to ask? Of course not. But there are a few things we will have to accept: 1) Finding a date can be as easy as simply looking up. 2) Our brain is a secondary character in our quest for love; our main job is to keep it from sabotaging our efforts. 3) Connecting on a date has less to do with being a sparkling conversationalist and more to do with staying in tune with our emotions and energy levels.

I came to these three conclusions after years of intense dating. As one friend put it, I earned my "PhD in dating"; however, I started out just like most introverts—admiring and fantasizing from afar. By my mid-twenties, I had had two or three real boyfriends and one short-lived marriage. But for the most part, my love life was about as eventful as a street party in the North Pole. Finally, I decided it was time to try out a different approach. Reeling from a recent breakup that I was having trouble getting over, I stumbled upon famous dating coach Rori Raye's blog. She advised accepting a date with any man who asked—that's right, *any* man. This actually didn't seem like that radical an idea since, despite my attractive appearance, I didn't get asked out very often.

Looking up to Find Love

The funny thing is, once I opened myself up to the idea of being asked out by anyone, the invitations started pouring in. Men approached me at the gym, at school, at work, and at the grocery store. Pretty much anywhere I went, men started noticing me and asking me out. Since then, I've realized that men had probably noticed me before I started dating en masse. It's just that I didn't notice them. I was like the woman in the famous Brazilian song "The Girl from Ipanema," which tells of a lovely young woman who goes walking by the sea. Her swaying hips and tan skin turn heads. One particular admirer smiles at her, but she doesn't notice because she is looking straight ahead. Perhaps she is going through her to-do list in her head.

Or maybe she's daydreaming about some handsome Brazilian guy she's been idolizing from afar. Whenever I hear that song, I wonder how many times I was oblivious to the gaze of a man who was just hoping that I would look up and notice him. On an average day, I didn't notice anything beyond the two feet of sidewalk in front of me.

We introverts tend to drift along in our bubble of fantasies (often thinking about our dream man or woman), oblivious to the real, live people right in front of us. We don't see the fellow introvert overthinking how to get our attention. If we look up, he might smile at us, and come up to say hello. Or we might see that a pretty girl has been eying us from across the room, hoping we might notice her. But we don't see her because we don't look up.

I have a friend who used to cross paths with a handsome man who walked his dog in her neighborhood. He always had his head down, and did not notice her. She was curious about him, but wasn't sure how to approach him. One day, she saw him walking right outside her workplace. She tried to get his attention, but, as usual, he was looking down and did not notice her. A little while later, she came across his familiar face on an online dating site. She sent him a message and he finally looked up long enough to read it. They've been together ever since. Imagine if my friend had not stumbled upon her handsome neighbor's online dating profile; they might never have met. It wouldn't have taken much effort for him to look up and notice that a beautiful woman was trying to get his attention. However, since he is an introvert, he kept his eyes and mind focused elsewhere and missed the first opportunities that were right in front of him.

The Brain Barrier

Before we can truly connect on a date, we must get past our greatest barrier to dating: our own minds. Overthinking is often what keeps us from making a move in the first place. It also prevents us from being open to the advances of another. Before we so much as make eye contact with someone we find attractive, we begin talking ourselves out of the whole thing. *What if she already has a partner?* we worry. Or we spend twenty minutes contemplating a guy's height and all the reasons we need a man who is at least three inches taller than us (hello, heels!). Meanwhile, Mr. Not-So-Tall starts chatting up a six-foot-tall Scandinavian woman who appears to have no qualms about their height difference.

The greatest lesson I learned during the several years it took me to earn my PhD in dating was that a date is really not that big of a deal. Some of us act as if a date is a marriage proposal. We begin contemplating living arrangements before we've even learned our suitor's last name. A date is merely a practice session. It is a casual swing of the bat in a game that will have countless strikeouts, and, if we're lucky, a few home runs. Many of us treat every date like it's the Super Bowl and we're about to announce our retirement. This might sound callous, but I swear it's true: eligible bachelors and bachelorettes are a renewable resource. When one swims away, another can come up just as quickly. But we won't notice fresh opportunity swimming our way unless we stop overthinking, ruminating, and worrying long enough to look up. Giving our brain a break from thinking about our exes helps too.

I once dated a guy who was firmly rooted in my social circle. We had mutual friends and frequented the same places.

This meant that after we broke up, we still crossed paths often. One night, while having dinner at a pub with one of my girl-friends, I saw through my peripheral vision that my ex had just walked in and was now sitting at the bar. Previously, I would have left the conversation to be with him, but I wouldn't have literally gotten up and walked to the bar. My mind would have done the walking. It would have floated right over to where my ex was sitting and hovered next to him for the rest of the evening. It would have contemplated his thoughts and feelings, and won-dered if he was thinking about me too. Instead, I decided to try something different on that occasion. I kept both my butt and my brain firmly planted in our booth. In other words, I stayed present with my friend. When I saw out of the corner of my eye that my ex was getting up to leave, I thought, *Let him go.* And that is precisely what I did. I didn't overthink his swift depar-ture, and what it all meant. I said a silent "sayonara" and went back to focusing on the lovely person right in front of me.

A few minutes after my ex left the bar, my friend got up to go to the bathroom. An attractive man took the opportunity to come over and introduce himself. "I noticed you the moment I walked in," he said. Even though I hadn't noticed him, I had, thankfully, looked up from the "ex fog" long enough for this man to see that I was approachable. He invited me to dinner and we ended up dating for a few weeks. It wasn't happily ever after; however, the experience served as a clear signpost point-ing me in the direction of love. The message was this: Stop ruminating about your ex and let someone new find you.

It's not just exes that cloud our thoughts and keep us from seeing the opportunities for love that are right in front of us. Like most humans, introverts have plenty of insecurities surrounding dating and relationships. All of our self-doubts rise to the surface the moment rejection is placed on the table. Nothing brings the possibility of rejection to the forefront of our mind like asking someone out on a date. Even if we are the one being asked out, the prospect of actually going on a date awakens insecurities we didn't even know we had.

One of our greatest worries is that we will not be able to find the right words. The fear of being tongue-tied is an ever-present challenge in an introvert's life. Dating shines a spotlight on our communication insecurities. We know it takes us a while to feel comfortable opening up to someone new. We also know that we are capable of having deep and meaningful conversations with our close friends. But our date probably won't know any of this. He is as clueless about us as we are about him or her. That's why we've forced ourselves to endure the discomfort of a first date—to get to know each other and find some connection points. Unfortunately, our brain is determined to thwart the whole process. Here is a sampling of some of the especially noisy thoughts that used to flail for my attention on a first date:

What if he thinks I'm too quiet? I should say something quick. Umm . . . hmmm . . . I don't know what to say. Oh, crap, now he's talking about the weather. This is bad . . . . Do I look uptight sitting like this? I should try to look more casual and relaxed; maybe slouch a little, but not too much. And what's my face doing? Uh oh, I'm doing that squinty thing with my eyes. I should smile more. Men like that. Just keep smiling . . . . Oh no, he's stopped talking. He's expecting me to comment on what he just shared. Shit, what did he just say? Something about his trip to Salmon Arm. Quick— say something about Salmon Arm! Ummm . . . hmm . . . I didn't think salmon had arms? No, not funny. Don't say that. Okay, he's starting to open up—this is good . . . . Oh no, not good, this guy has a lot of baggage. Maybe this was a bad idea. Maybe I should listen to my mother and start dating younger men . . .

My mind was so crowded with unnecessary judgments and worries that I couldn't relax. It's hard to open up and "be yourself" when our mind is in overdrive; yet, this is exactly how most introverts approach a first date. We wind our worries round and round until we are completely constricted by our own thoughts. Then we wonder why we can't just relax and play it cool.

Let's explore a common dating scenario and play a little game of what not to do on a first date. See if you can spot where Cyndi and Jake go wrong:

Cyndi has a date with Jake, a guy she met through an online dating site. She's excited and nervous because she has high hopes for this one. He seems like perfect boyfriend material. He's handsome, has a good job as an engineer, and loves animals. Plus, it says in his profile that he is looking for a serious relationship. As she gets ready for the date, Cyndi worries about what they will talk about. She is an introvert and sometimes doesn't know what to say. She hopes there won't be any awkward silences.

During the date, Cyndi discovers that Jake is shorter than she imagined. She is disappointed. She also finds out that Jake likes to play hockey twice a week (he is from Canada). This concerns Cyndi because she doesn't normally connect with jock types. She also worries that he won't make time for her if he's always out playing sports or watching games on TV.

Jake tells Cyndi many stories about all the places he's traveled to and the exciting things he's done. Cyndi is a little bored, but happy that Jake is carrying the conversation. At the end of the date, they hug and thank each other for a "lovely evening." Neither can tell if the other is actually interested. They never see each other again.

There are several ways that Cyndi and Jake let their minds get in the way of true connection. Cyndi does what many introverts do before a date. She thinks about what could go wrong. Perhaps even more detrimental to the date are her thoughts about what could go right. Cyndi is already imagining a future with a man she has only interacted with online. It doesn't help that Cyndi has high expectations for the date. Her high hopes multiply both her fantasies and her apprehensions. This creates a lot of tension within Cyndi before she even steps out the door.

Once Cyndi has projected her fantasies far enough into the future, she's back to imagining worst-case scenarios again. While on the date, Cyndi worries that Jake's love of sports might one day overshadow his love for her. Never mind that she doesn't yet know if they have chemistry or can enjoy each other's company.

Cyndi evaluates Jake with the impersonal eye of a test examiner. Everything Jake says gets a pass or fail. It's stressful having someone silently assess your every move. While I was trying on various programs and careers in my early twenties, I spent a year studying dental hygiene. During my clinical training, my instructors were constantly evaluating everything I did—and I mean *everything*—from the way I wiped down my chair to the precise placement of my fingers on my instruments. To this day, I remember those evaluations as the most stressful experiences of my life. Feeling like we are being evaluated on a first date is nearly as nerve-racking. Most of us react in one of two ways: we strive to prove ourselves to our evaluator, or we shut down. Jake chooses the former by trying to impress Cyndi with his travel stories. The moment we try to prove or even justify ourselves on a first date, we stifle true connection.

The interaction is no longer about sharing and relating. It is about getting an A+ on our evaluation, even if that means boring our date in the process.

Unzipping the Armor

Neither Cyndi nor Jake give any indication as to whether or not they like the other person. It's as though they are back in grade school, trying to keep their affections a secret. For introverts who are used to admiring from afar, it's easy to forget that it's okay to show others how we feel.

Being fully present with our feelings and sensations helps us bypass our noisy brain and relax into the moment while we're on a date. Whenever I go on a date, I do a little visualization I learned from Rori Raye. I imagine myself unzipping an invisible armor over my chest. I open my heart and let all the worries and judgments melt away. Every time I start to feel nervous, I take a deep breath and bring my attention to my physical senses. I take in the scene around me. I relax into my body and feel the sensation of the wind on my skin. I notice the scent of a familiar cologne drifting my way.

While on the date, I make a conscious effort to notice and express my emotions. This doesn't mean that I dive straight into my greatest fears and insecurities on a first date. That level of vulnerability wouldn't match the circumstances. Instead, I allow whomever I'm with to catch a glimpse of what I'm feeling in that moment, whether that be excitement, nervousness, or even a little bit of grouchiness. The point is that I let my date see past the armor. I give him a peek at the French lace of my soul; just a peek is often enough. The moment I started expressing more emotion on dates, I noticed an instant shift in how men reacted to me. They started really looking at me. They saw past the pretty face and connected with the person underneath. It's reassuring to know that revealing the essence of my emotions is more important than wearing the perfect outfit or coming up with a bunch of smart-sounding questions to prevent awkward silences. I was also pleased to find that conversations became more interesting as men began to feel comfortable sharing their true feelings and opinions too.

If you are a man and you're wondering if expressing more feelings on a date will make you seem wussy, I invite you to observe a machismo Latino in action. Because of my extensive travels in Latin America, I was able to experience the Latino approach to seduction first hand. Most men I encountered there were not afraid to say or show how they felt. If they were angry, happy, sad, or horny, they were sure to say so without a hint of embarrassment. Their ability to express exactly how they felt at any given moment showed confidence. No matter which emotion they were wearing, they made it look masculine by donning it with pride. Introverted men can do this in a more subtle way. Quietly saying "I feel happy right now," is as much an invitation for connection as shouting it would be.

Energy Awareness on a Date

Understanding and managing our energy levels while dating is crucial for introverts. All the overwhelming sensations we feel while socializing is multiplied when on a date. Not only do we have to spend time with someone we barely know, we also have to engage in nonstop conversation with them. As we discussed in a previous chapter, conversations are draining for introverts. Even listening can leave us feeling exhausted. When we are talking to our close friends, pauses are nothing to worry about. On the other hand, when we are sitting face to face with a hot date, we feel a lot of pressure to avoid even a few seconds of silence. On a date, the game of conversation plays out at peak intensity. We feel the need to keep the ball in the air at all times, even if we would rather throw down our racket and take a really long water break. This is why I recommend choosing dates where a one-on-one conversation is not the main event. I've gone for walks, bike rides, and boat rides on first dates. I've even gone stand-up paddleboarding. Since I find nature energizing, doing a casual outdoor activity counteracts the inevitable energy drain of dating.

As with any social activity, it's best to go into a date with an escape plan. Walks are great because they can be shortened or lengthened depending on how we are feeling. Long hiking loops are usually not a good idea for a first date. It's no fun running out of energy and conversation topics before you even reach the midway point of a three-hour hike. Coffee dates are also easy to escape, but they do require constant conversation. I could be biased because I don't actually like coffee, but I find going on coffee dates beyond boring. I know others who wouldn't dare do anything else on a first date. The key is to tailor our dating activities to suit our personal preferences and energy levels.

Paying attention to our energy levels on a date is also important for determining compatibility. I used to go into dates with a checklist, listening carefully to see if a man could tick all the boxes. Now, I've realized that the checklist means nothing if my date makes me feel drained. Sometimes, it's hard to tell whether it is the person making us feel tired or the circumstances. This is where our introverted intuition is a real asset. It helps to make note of how we physically feel while conversing with our date. Ask yourself: Is their tension in my throat? Do my eyes feel heavy? Do I feel light and happy or heavy and frazzled?

After dating a variety of personality types, I've noticed that, in general, I feel more drained if I'm on a date with an extrovert. Of course, there are always exceptions. Jared, whom I mentioned in Chapter Three, made me feel energized when we first started dating, so much so that it would take me days to come down from my Jared high. I now see that the jolt of energy Jared gave me was too jarring for my sensitive constitution. On the other hand, I have dated extroverts who have had less of an impact on my energy levels. I've since realized that it all comes down to pacing. If my extroverted date approaches conversation and socializing at a similar pace to mine, then I don't feel overwhelmed.

The advantage of dating fellow introverts is that they often match our stride when socializing. They naturally ease into slower, more in-depth conversations. They understand the beauty of an empty social calendar. I have, however, dated introverts who loved to pack their schedule with social events. Their need for constant activity exhausted me.

In the end, our energy levels are a better indicator of compatibility than introversion or extroversion. Paying attention to how our date impacts our energy will give us a glimpse into the potential future of the relationship. If we feel drained after a thirty-minute conversation with a person, thirty years of marriage will likely turn us into the walking dead. On the other hand, if we can spend a whole day with someone and feel energized, we can start to imagine spending the rest of our life with that person.

Online Dating for Introverts

Many people suggest that online dating is the ideal way for introverts to find love. It certainly does have its advantages. Since most introverts express themselves better in writing than in person, cyber dialogue can be the perfect segue into real-life dating. Online dating also allows introverts to minimize approach anxiety. It's a lot easier to ask someone out in writing than face-to-face. Likewise, rejection is easier to stomach when it is done via instant message.

It's not just online dating sites that make cyber match-making possible. An introverted client of mine met his current girlfriend on Pinterest. They had been commenting on the same post, and eventually decided to take their conversation to a more private domain (pun intended). I'm sure there are plenty of introverts out there who met their partners through online forums, Facebook groups, and various other social media platforms.

Of course, online dating does have its disadvantages. I have done my fair share of cyber dating, and after a while, I started to feel like I was commodifying people. One man wrote "Add to Cart" as his profile tagline, and I laughed out loud (LOL'd) at the irony. We're searching for a soul mate, yet we view potential matches more like products rather than people. I've also noticed that a lot of people never make it past the keyboard conversations. Rather than use online dating as a segue into in-person interactions, they use it to *avoid* real-life connection. They never make the leap from texting to talking, so their relationships fizzle out before they even begin. In my experience, the best way to approach online dating is to view it as a bridge toward in-person meetings. It's okay to inch our way across, or even spend some time lingering in the middle, but eventually we'll have to cross over to the other side and actually go on a real date.

As you begin taking swings at the bat by going on real, live, face-to-face dates, remember that you bring many strengths to the table as an introvert. Curious and attentive introverts make great companions, whether that be for a short stroll through a local park or a meandering journey through the peaks and valleys of life. Most introverts are looking for the right person with whom to do the latter. We want an intimate relationship with someone who will appreciate our loyal love. In the next chapter, we'll discuss how introverts can cultivate more intimate and fulfilling relationships.

14

Introverted Intimacy

"My feeling at the end is that AA is utterly amazing.
Complete strangers getting together in rooms at all hours
and saying things that are so personal, so incredibly intimate.
This is the kind of stuff that happens in a relationship
after a few months. But people here open up right away,
with everyone. It's like some sort of love affair, stripped
of the courtship phase. I feel bathed in safety."

—*Augusten Burroughs,* Dry

Alcoholics Anonymous is not the place one would expect to find fulfilling companionship. Yet, Burroughs's description of a typical AA meeting describes an introvert's fantasy for friendship. We want to skip the preamble and go straight to the important stuff. I've often told people (while lamenting one mangled romance or another) that I wish I could just jump into the middle of a relationship. This goes for both romantic relationships and friendships. Beginnings are so uncomfortable. New relationships are like the shock of bright light and cold floors first thing in the morning. We know there are good things to be had in the day ahead, but our beds feel so warm and safe. Ideally, we would bring our blanket cocoons with us as we ease into the day. This is how we would like our relationships to begin. We want to slide right in without any annoying small talk. At the same time, we want to be swaddled in the security that comes with being in the center of something.

A while ago I watched a documentary called *Twinsters*. It is about South Korean twin sisters who were adopted at birth and raised oceans apart (one in France and one in the US). The twins didn't know about the other's existence until the French sister saw her own face staring back at her in a YouTube video. Only, it was not her; it was her long-lost twin, who now lives in Los Angeles. When the twins reconnected, they felt as though they had known each other their whole lives. They held hands as they walked, giggled over their similarities, and talked late into the night. The French twin, who happens to be an introvert, admitted that she had often felt lonely as a child but didn't want to play with other children. Her heart longed for the twin sister she didn't know existed.

A lot of introverts can relate to the sense that we are missing someone whom we have never met. When we are lonely, not anyone will do. We want our other half and our twin soul, or, at the very least, someone who understands us and accepts us for who we are. We would prefer if this relationship just fell into our lap the way it did for the sisters in *Twinsters*. As sisters, the twins knew that theirs was a bond worth investing in. Introverts are usually reluctant to invest in a person until we know we will receive some kind of return on our investment. The returns we're most interested in are soulful conversations, comfortable silences, shared experiences, and our own versions of fun. We are all too aware that we won't find this kind of connection with just anyone.

Introverts are like a light switch when it comes to both our hobbies and our people. We are either completely obsessed and "turned on" (not necessarily in a sexual sense) by something or someone, or we are totally switched off and disinterested. My Egyptian friend Moe, whom I mentioned before, tells me that there is no Arabic equivalent for the word "like." This caused some confusion when he first arrived in Canada as an adolescent. Without the word "like" to balance things out, the pendulum of his emotional expressions swung to two extremes: love and hate. He loved mangoes. He loved snow. He loved our sour-faced English teacher who always looked like she had just swallowed a glass of salt water. He hated peanut butter. Introverts are like this. We have no internal vocabulary for "like." We are either utterly enamored and obsessed, or we don't care. If someone sparks our interest, we want to know what fills their internal bookshelf. If we really like them, we want to climb right inside their head and pull the biggest book we can find off the shelf. If there is no spark, we'd rather reread some volumes from our own collection.

The Fear of Getting Closer

Many introverts have so much pain associated with intimacy that we are afraid to get close. There is the pain of being emotionally overwhelmed. The pain of moving too quickly. The pain of being misunderstood and feeling like the bad guy all the time. Then, of course, there is the pain of knowing that we are causing someone else pain simply by fulfilling our innate needs. Our partner feels our need for space as a slap in the face. Our lack of energy is interpreted as a lack of love. All of these pain associations make us reluctant to get close, no matter how much we say we want a meaningful relationship.

You might have heard of the hedgehog's dilemma, a concept outlined by the German philosopher Arthur Schopenhauer in 1851. Hedgehogs want to huddle together to share warmth in the winter, but must remain apart to avoid hurting one another with their sharp spines. This is a metaphor for the ultimate dilemma in human intimacy: Get close and hurt one another, or stay apart and feel lonely.

Most people have some fears surrounding intimacy. The two most common fears people have in relationships are engulfment and abandonment. Usually, it is one or the other. We fear being swallowed up by another and dissolving into the relationship. Or, we fear the opposite—we are terrified of being left behind. The introvert's dilemma in relationships is that we often feel both fears deeply. We are on constant guard against the threat of being overwhelmed by others. And yet, we are afraid that our true personalities will scare people away. Our worst fear is that we are too easy to leave, which might mean we are too hard to love. It is as if we are afraid of the sun, but also afraid of the sun setting. I wrote a poem about this a while ago:

Fear of the sun
And fear of the sun setting
Engulfment
Abandonment
The sun's rays reach for me
But the once welcome warmth
Now burns
The moon in all its glowing mystery
Can't be trusted
It calls to the stars in the dark
Circles the world

Like a predator its prey
It shows you a sliver
Then disappears for days

For sensitive introverts who are prone to energy drain, relationships can feel like swimming in a tsunami. The tidal wave of emotions, the silent fears, the rush of hormones, the sheer weight of someone else's expectations—it can all be too much. Whenever I think of one of my extroverted exes, a particular image comes to mind. I imagine that I am a little blue bird in the palm of his hands. He is trying to show me affection, but ends up smothering me with his large clumsy hands. This is what engulfment feels like to an introvert. Hold us too tightly and we'll collapse into ourselves, disappearing into our own world. The alternative is that we literally disappear. We become the abandoner. Often, the person who needs us too much will be the person we run from. Brenda Knowles, creator, writer and personal coach of BrendaKnowles.com explains:

> Neediness is my dating kryptonite. If I sense someone needs their hand held constantly or is a possessive type, I run like the wind. That kind of relationship requires a lot of external attention, which, no matter how exciting at first, ends up being a drain.
>
> Constant drama and complaining will also leave me as lifeless as a forgotten doll. Deep empathy is another trait of many introverts. If you have problems/pain in your life, I will feel for you intensely. I will want to help/show you light, which is all fine and good until I find myself in the dark with nothing left to give.

Sometimes, we run because we feel like we don't have enough to offer. We believe our value is measured by quantity (how much we say, do, or achieve), instead of quality. Extroverts bring a lot of social capital to relationships, exposing introverts to new people and activities. On top of this, extroverts have *enthusiasm*, one of the most celebrated (and overrated) qualities of the twenty-first century. They also have plenty of energy for doing, planning, and organizing. While introverts feel overwhelmed just thinking about a packed social calendar, extroverts cheer, "Bring it on!" The other thing about extroverts is that they get us out of our shell. They are the ones who reach out to us with open palms, and say, "C'mon, let's have an adventure." Sometimes this is annoying, but we are often thankful for the invitation. All of this might seem more significant than what we pitch in. We barely acknowledge the wealth of positive qualities we offer in a relationship. Sure, we are loyal, patient, reliable, and grounded, but what does that matter? Surely, social capital is more valuable than what we bring to the table. It's easy to forget that our extroverts also appreciate our shell. They don't like it so much when it blocks them out, but they enjoy crawling inside our protective armor with us once in a while. They feel safe with us.

The role introverts play in a relationship might be different than that of an extrovert, but it is just as important. I recently took up AcroYoga, a form of partner yoga with acrobatic elements. In AcroYoga, one person takes on the role of "base," and one person is the "flyer." The base supports the flyer, as he or she does aerial postures. In other words, the flyer does the bending, twisting, and flying through the air, while the base pretty much just lies there like a human launchpad (at least, that's what it looks like on the outside). At first, I couldn't fathom why anyone would enjoy being a base. The flyer role looked more fun and impressive. But when I actually tried out basing, I realized how rewarding it is. Basing makes you feel grounded and powerful, or, as my instructor puts it, "totally badass." Likewise, introverts can and should feel good about the role we play in relationships, even if it doesn't seem impressive at first glance.

For some introverts, just the idea of partnership has us sweating. Letting someone in means letting go of a portion of our precious independence. The thought of depending on someone else worries us. It's not that we don't want support; we do! It's just that, in the past, relying on others left us feeling more ragged than relieved. The thing is, we know that there is always give-and-take in relationships. We worry that when our turn to take comes along, we won't have anything to give in return, at least not on a consistent basis. What if the person needs us when we are at a painfully low, hide-in-the-blankets-all-day point in our energy cycle?

We might also worry about becoming too dependent on a particular person. Since we have few close relationships, we naturally expect more from the people in our inner circle. Sometimes, our circle can get so small that we expect one person to fulfill all of our needs. We count on our partner or BFF (best friend forever) to supply constant companionship, affection, love, entertainment, and validation. That is a lot of pressure to put on one person. When our friend or partner feels burdened, we feel guilty. This is a recipe for conflict.

Many introverts avoid such conflicts by opting out of close relationships altogether. This is one solution. But a better option might be to learn how to accept support, while also carrying our own weight. Going back to the example of AcroYoga, bases never feel like they are carrying the full weight of the flyer. This is because the flyer doesn't just flop down on the base like a rag doll. She carefully positions herself so that the base's strongest points carry the brunt of her weight. She also uses her own muscles to hold herself up. We introverts can do the same in our relationships. We can be supported, while also drawing on our own strengths to reach new heights.

Our Hearts Cross Paths

Over the years, I've discovered that the number one indicator of whether or not I will get close to someone is not a similar background, temperament, or even shared interests. It is proximity. I wish I could say that it is something more mysterious and magical than this. If someone hangs out on my patch of grass long enough, I soften to him or her, and vice versa. Our masks start to melt away, and we begin to see one another for who we really are. The authentic versions of two people are bound to be more intimate than the puffed-up garden party versions. As much as I try to be myself up front, sometimes I need a second (or twenty-second) chance to make an authentic first impression. Proximity makes this possible.

I have a friend whom I bump into a lot while running errands. The last time I ran into him at the library, he said something in Thai, which, of course, I didn't understand. "Our hearts cross paths," he explained. "It's a Thai saying." What a lovely way to view chance encounters. Living in proximity to someone allows our hearts to cross paths often. This is probably why one of my most emotionally intimate relationships was with a roommate. We were just friends, but over time, sharing dinners and sharing space created trust. The walls came down and we started sharing things that were scarier to express: dreams that seemed too grandiose to admit, feelings that weren't so pretty, kind words that we feared wouldn't be reciprocated. In other words, we started being vulnerable with one another. If we had not lived together, I'm certain we would never have become so close. Proximity and time allowed us to inch our way into intimacy.

It turns out that research backs up my personal belief in the power of proximity. Research has shown that physical proximity promotes closer relationships. A study by Festinger, Schachter, and Back explored how friendships formed among college students who lived in married student housing at Massachusetts Institute of Technology. They found that the closest friendships were forged among students who lived on the same floor or in the same dormitory. They also found that students living on a lower floor near a stairwell were more likely than their neighbors to befriend students living on the floor above. They concluded that repeated chance meetings lead to friendship. Proximity helps promote such encounters.

The longer we live in proximity with someone, the more likely we are to become close. This is good news for introverts who feel more comfortable letting relationships unfold slowly; however, not everyone appreciates the slow approach to intimacy. Nowadays, many people are as quick to exchange bodily fluids as they are to exchange phone numbers. In my experience, the relationships that form most rapidly disintegrate just as fast. If we make time and proximity our allies, building close relationships is less jarring. The stress is spread out over many meetings instead of falling, like an avalanche, on the first encounter. Less stress means more room for pleasure. We can actually start enjoying the process of getting closer.

Of course, this doesn't mean that simply anyone we encounter often enough will become a friend for life. If familiarity reveals annoying or detestable qualities in a person, we probably won't want to get close to them. I can recall several past roommates who've proved this point to me. I like to think of it this way: if our true self is compatible with another person's true self, proximity and time will help us get past the bullshit long enough to connect. What a relief this revelation is for introverts!

So much of the anxiety we feel surrounding intimacy has to do with pacing. Society expects us to move at a velocity that is out of whack with our internal speedometer for getting close. We want to take the scenic route to intimacy, stopping along the way to lie in the grass or dip our toes in the ocean. Physical intimacy is no different.

Studies have shown that introverts have fewer sexual partners than extroverts. In his book *Sex and Personality*, psychologist Hans Eysenck explores how personality influences sexual behavior. His findings show that extroverts have more sex, and they do so in more varied positions and with more partners than introverts. As you can see, *more* is the operative word when it comes to extroverts and sex. Of course, this doesn't mean that all extroverts are running around like randy rabbits looking for their next shag. And it certainly doesn't mean that introverts are inexperienced lovers who rarely have sex. What it does indicate is that extroverts and introverts tend to approach sex differently. For introverts, too much too soon is stressful. Far from the meandering scenic route we long for, sex early on feels more like teleportation to introverts. One minute we are carrying on in familiar surroundings, and the next our body materializes in another person's bedroom. Physically we are here, but emotionally we are not. We want to spend more time traversing the breezy meadows of friendship before easing into physical intimacy. I'm sure there are plenty of introverts out there who have one-night stands and who (gasp!) really do enjoy it. If this is the case for you, more power to you. But for many introverts, sex before emotional intimacy is at best unfulfilling, and at worst totally mortifying.

No matter how much we stretch out the get-to-know-you process, there will always be points in a relationship when we must take little leaps into the unknown. These points show up like a fork in the road that offers us two choices: be honest or just say "I'm fine" and move on; admit to others how we feel or play it cool; let another person into our messy homes and our even messier hearts or keep the door shut. There is so much uncertainty when faced with these kinds of choices. We don't know if we'll be rejected and come off as fools, or if the person we let in will break things. We take the risk in the hopes that they will tread gently and make the place lovelier than before.

That's another thing about AcroYoga—just like in relationships, there is an element of risk. I noticed when I was basing for the first time that there is a moment of uncertainty right before you enter a posture with your partner. This fraction of a second of unknowns is both thrilling and terrifying. As the base, you don't know if the connection is solid enough for you to lift your partner. As the flyer, you don't know if you can trust that the base won't drop you. If the connection is off, one or both of you could get hurt. But there is another possibility: you can both face those few milliseconds of uncertainty with complete trust, and create a partnership that soars.

I See You

The true foundation of intimacy is to be able to see, and feel seen. In her book *The Art of Asking: Or How I Learned to Stop Worrying and Let People Help*, which I mentioned in Chapter One, Amanda Palmer talks about her time as a street performer. She would dress up as a bride statue and offer flowers to those who gave her money. Each time she handed out a flower, she locked eyes with her patron. Her steady gaze said, "I see you." Palmer was amazed by the intimate moments that occurred as a result of something as simple as prolonged eye contact. Her art facilitated a quiet moment in a busy world, allowing two strangers to feel seen.

It might help to remember the above scene as you seek more depth in your relationships. The true objective is simply to see: see another person for who they really are, flaws and all; see yourself with more compassion as you recognize that this person is just as afraid as you are; see the value of something as basic as looking a person in the eye. As you do this, hopefully, you will also see that you already have everything you need to get close to another.

You are already irresistible.

Acknowledgments

First and foremost, I want to acknowledge my amazing "innie community." It is thanks to the countless introverts around the world who read my blog, *Introvert Spring*, and weekly newsletter that this book is possible. I am especially grateful to my clients and students, who helped me develop many of the concepts in this book.

My editor, Kimberley Lim, at Skyhorse deserves a big thank you for believing in this little book from the beginning, and giving it a nip and tuck in all the right places. I would also like to express my sincere appreciation to Barbara Florio-Graham for her guidance on finalizing the contract for this book. My grandmother and fellow author, Sylvia Adams, has been a huge supporter of my writing from the start, as has my mother, Jane. You told me I could do anything, and I actually believed you. Thank you.

I'd also like to tip my hat to John, Shelley, and the "lucky house" where I signed this contract, as well as all of those crazy individuals spread out across the globe, from Mexico to Australia, who believed in me when I was just a vagabond with a dream. *Mil gracias.*

A Note from the Author

Before I was an author, I was a blogger. I would love it if you joined the hundreds of thousands of introverts from around the world who follow my blog, *Introvert Spring*. There is a wealth of free resources on the site, as well as on my various social media platforms.

How to Find More of My Introvert Resources:

STEP 1: Visit my website, www.introvertspring.com, and enter your email address to get two free ebooks and free articles I don't share on the site.

STEP 2: Like my Introvert Spring Facebook page so you never miss a thing. I regularly share introvert articles, memes, cartoons, and infographics on the page, which has tens of thousands of followers.

STEP 3: Navigate to the resources section of my website and check out my introvert courses and virtual workshops. These courses have been created with the specific challenges and strengths of introverts in mind. I'd love to be your guide in building confidence and connections the introverted way.